Faith, Serpents, and Fire

Images of Kentucky Holiness Believers

Faith,

Images of Kentucky Holiness Believers

Scott W. Schwartz

Serpents, and Fire

University Press
of Mississippi / Jackson

Copyright © 1999
by University Press of Mississippi

All rights reserved

Manufactured in Canada

02 01 00 99   4 3 2 1

Library of Congress Cataloging-in-
Publication Data

Schwartz, Scott W.
    Faith, serpents, and fire : images of
Kentucky Holiness believers / Scott
W. Schwartz.
      p. cm.
    Includes bibliographical references.
    ISBN 1-57806-092-3 (cloth : alk.
paper)
      1. Snake cults (Holiness churches)
—Kentucky. 2. Kentucky—Religious
life and customs. 1. Title.
BX7990.H6S38 1999
289.9—dc21

                        98–28471
                          CIP

British Library Cataloging-in-Publication
Data available

Frontis: Punkin Brown, True Tabernacle
of Jesus Christ (Middlesboro, Kentucky,
August 3, 1996), serpent handling

To my beautiful family,
Sarah, Samantha, Aaron, and Kathryn,
for their constant love and support,
and to all children of Appalachia

Contents

Foreword

A common experience among those who witness the ritual handling of serpents and fire by Christian believers is that of a shared epiphany. Although they may not find the same meanings in these events, participants and observers alike often intuitively grasp profound perceptions of reality. From the first days of the practice in the early part of this century, for example, numerous accounts record that many of those who came scoffing left praying.

Scott Schwartz did not go scoffing to the services of Holiness serpent and fire handlers, but he went at first with considerable curiosity. That curiosity was soon converted into scientific inquiry and then into humanistic and philosophical perception.

One of the principal questions confronting any nonparticipant is "What does this ritual mean?" From one perspective, its meaning lies in the mind of the beholder. Whether all the varied responses of the multiple minds would be considered truth depends upon the criteria for truth. But, adapting the criteria suggested by Alfred, Lord Tennyson for the analysis of poetry, one might say that the ritual is "shot-silk with many glancing colours," and that each individual "must find his own interpretation according to his ability, and according to his sympathy" with the participant.

Scott Schwartz brings to his analysis of these "signs-following" Christians not only informed analytical faculties but also a sensitivity which allows him to enter objectively into the feelings and actions of others.

Schwartz's data on fire handling help to map largely uncharted waters; his analysis of the music provides an expanded vista of an integral component of the services; and his photographs are studies within themselves. But his focus—an important one in understanding Holiness serpent and fire handlers—is on the fact that the people are believers. Whatever else may be said about the intellectual, psychological, and cultural factors involved, these "signs . . . follow them that believe." Whether the meaning lies in the realm of the divine spirit or of the physical body, it emanates from belief. There may be greater virtues, but faith certainly remains part of a celebrated triumvirate.

Thomas Burton

Acknowledgments

When I was a young child, my grandmother once said to me, "Before you judge anyone, you must walk a mile in their shoes." The meaning of these simple words continues to resonate, a gentle reminder from a time long past that I must always remain open-minded regarding ideas and beliefs that I might not understand. This single admonition has enabled me to look beyond the shallow prejudices of one culture and seek out what is beautiful in another. Without those sage words, I could never have written this book.

The images and words in this volume document a people's most sacred beliefs. Their willingness to allow me to explore the depths of their faith and religious practice provided me with countless learning opportunities. Because they were patient with my endless questioning while I was visiting in their homes and churches, I was able to gain knowledge and understanding that would not have been possible through the reading of books alone. Sherman, Valerie, Gary, Kimberly, Wayne, Sheila, Bruce, Jamie, Carl, Brenda, Buffy, Billy, Bertha, and the many other wonderful individuals too numerous to list—thank you. I am eternally grateful for the opportunities you have given me and the friendships I have developed with you over the years. Punkin Brown, a kind and generous man, thank you for your time and candor. I will miss your warm smile and laugh. Your father's words at the funeral October 8, 1998 give me strength in the knowledge that "you fought the good fight and are now with Melinda and your Lord."

The 1960s lyric "I get by with a little help from my friends" sums up my feelings regarding the tremendous amount of assistance my colleagues have given me. Without Ann Kuebler's gentle insistence, I would have never found my "voice" and would still be churning out the same stale prose that could bring sleep even to the hardcore insomniac. The staff of East Tennessee State University's Center for Appalachian Studies and Services always managed to provide some funding and equipment whenever it seemed that the project was about to come to a standstill. I could not have gotten through any of this without Charles Moore's great sense of humor and his oversized couch. Special thanks must be given to Blair White and the staff of the B. Carroll Reece Museum for taking a risk on an unknown photographer and producing my first photography exhibit. Dr. Reid Blackwelder and Dr. Kenneth Ferslew deserve a special note of thanks for taking time from their busy schedules at the medical school to shepherd me through the scientific study, and so does my father, Ronald Schwartz, for helping fund the study when the grant money was suddenly pulled from the project. My fellow Appalachian researchers David Kimbrough, Ralph Hood, John Boles, and members of the Appalachian Studies Association gave me much guidance. My director, John Fleckner, has been one of my strongest supporters at the Smithsonian Institution (no small effort given his complete dislike of serpents). My editor, Craig Gill, has been an absolute delight and has always "gently" pushed me in a direction that assured the success of this project. I am grateful to Tom Burton, one of the best scholars I have had the pleasure to work with and, fortunately for me, a good friend. The Virginia Railway Express deserves a special thank you—the book could never have been written without those long and consistent delays. I send special thanks also to the Harlan Dairy Queen, where the coffee was always hot and strong.

Finally, to my gorgeous Sarah—my chief editor, friend, partner in crime, and main squeeze—for your understanding about all those times I was away from home and for your constant support, I send thanks from the bottom of my heart.

Faith, Serpents, and Fire

Images of Kentucky Holiness Believers

Introduction

Ashort time after I began working as the technical services archivist for East Tennessee State University's Archives of Appalachia in 1989, Tom Burton asked me if I could help him define the music of the Appalachian serpent handlers for a book that he was writing for the University of Tennessee Press. After spending several weeks listening to and transcribing music that he had recorded during some West Virginia and Kentucky church services, I was unable to provide him with any helpful information. My difficulty was not in interpreting the specific features of the music but rather in understanding the context of the church service and the role this music played during the services. After listening to my observations, Tom handed me a videotape of a Baxter, Kentucky, service from 1985 and suggested that it might provide me with a context for understanding this music. The tape contained scenes of Sherman Ward handling fire; it was the first time I had seen such a practice, and it convinced me to continue my research on the music of the Appalachian serpent and fire handlers.

I spent the next two years viewing more of Tom's field recordings and reading, but I was unable to find a church that would allow me to videotape and photograph their serpent-handling services. In August 1992 Tom invited me to attend a homecoming service in Middlesboro, Kentucky. He had previously recorded the members of this church, and they were willing to allow me to do the same. To my surprise, Sherman Ward, whom I had watched handle fire on a videotape two years earlier, was participating in this service.

3

The church service resembled many others that I had viewed on the videotapes. After the service everyone walked to a picnic that was being set up behind the church. During this picnic I introduced myself to Sherman and asked him and his son numerous questions about their fire-handling experiences. We spent nearly an hour talking about their spiritual experiences, but they did not extend an invitation to attend, videotape, and photograph one of their church services.

As we walked to the parking lot, Sherman noticed that he had a flat tire on his van and said that, because of a back injury, he was not able to change the tire himself. I offered to help, and, along with Mark Ray, a member of Sherman's Ross Point church, quickly replaced the tire. Sherman then invited me to attend and record one of his church services the following month. His only request was that he and the members of the church receive a copy of the videotape.

This book is the result of the many visits that I made to Sherman's church between 1992 and 1995, as well as to the churches of Jamie Coots and Bruce Helton between 1992 and 1996. The essays and photographs are meant to provide a series of impressions and images of activities in these churches where serpent handling is part of the service. I don't attempt to explain either the meaning of this religious practice or its impact throughout Appalachia; the book is intended to be an introduction to three "Jesus Only"[1] churches in eastern Kentucky and to the social and spiritual interactions that typically occur during these services.

The photographs were taken with 35mm, 400 ASA film, without flash, in an effort to intrude as little as possible upon the services. As a result, the film was "push-processed" two and three stops. The pronounced grain and the strident patterns of light in these images are the result of this process and of my desire to have the photographs represent the mood of the spiritual experiences. The photographs and essays record the complex and sometimes humorous social interactions that I encountered and provide an intimate glimpse into serpent-handling practices and beliefs, moving beyond the stereotypes of Appalachian snake charmers and fire eaters to illustrate the deeply personal and communal spirituality that is an integral element of the services.[2]

Glad Tidings

The trip is familiar—left at Duffield, right to Pennington Gap, and right again to Harlan, Kentucky. Route 421 is the worst part of the drive. It snakes through Virginia's and Kentucky's mountains past one-stop gas marts, red brick houses, abandoned coal tipples, and three small faded crosses nailed to a tree. The sun is sliding behind the mountains. Approaching the final hairpin curve into Crummies, Kentucky, I switch on the headlights and look up from the dashboard just in time to avoid hitting a coal truck doing some overtime.

I pull into the church's small parking lot, and the preacher's wife, Valerie, waves to me as she walks into the church.[3] The white cinder-block-and-wood building stands next to a row of redbud trees that have been stripped of their weathered leaves by January's unrelenting winds. I take in a deep breath and think to myself, "Kentucky is a much prettier place in the spring."

I'm greeted by the familiar odor of blazing kerosene heaters as I walk through the front door. Bags of recording and photographic equipment hang from my shoulders like giant supply sacks and make me look like a yuppie peddler. I shake hands with several of my new friends and sit down in a worn wooden pew. Biblical quotations, a wooden cross, and images of Christ are carefully displayed on each wall. Only a phosphorus-colored clock with the word "Squirt" stenciled across its face seems out of place. Kerosene-filled Coke bottles, a propane torch, and a bottle of olive oil have been set on the pulpit. A worn Bible is opened to Mark

Grays Knob, Kentucky, Route 421
(September 23, 1995)

5

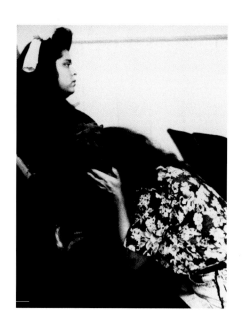

Valerie Ward and Buffy Helton, True Tabernacle of Jesus Christ (Middlesboro, Kentucky, August 22, 1993), praying

16, verses 17–18, in preparation for the night's salvation. Handcrafted boxes lie beneath the front pew, and a sporadic buzzing is the only hint of the serpents inside. Nothing has changed since last month's visit.

As I begin setting up equipment, my mind drifts for a moment. Why am I doing this? The answer comes to me in a flash of images as I open up my tripod. Men and women greeting each other as brother and sister in the church's dusty parking lot, the men exchanging handshakes, the women herding the children into the meeting house, sitting down next to the serpent boxes, and showing one another the latest photographs of their children and grandchildren. Sherman standing outside the church talking with Gary and Wayne about hunting deer with his son in Boone County on a sunny afternoon. Kimberly taking a well-practiced snap of a hickory switch to her son's backside to stop him from running inside the church. A young girl sitting next to her sister and flirting with some pubescent boys. Everything seems so natural; yet the media's blitz about a recent serpent-handling fatality paints a much darker and more sinister picture of these people. However, I am drawn by a brighter image.

No one seems to notice that I'm back for the Saturday service. Reaching for my video camera, I notice a tired-looking man sitting with his two daughters, one sleeping next to him and the other merrily chattering to her grandmother. Jesus's name is tattooed across the knuckles of his left hand, the tattoo having been created with blue ink and a nail.

I look at my watch and notice that it is 7:06 p.m. Gary and Wayne have settled down behind the pulpit, tuning their guitars. Matt picks a finger-blazing "riff" aimed at no one in particular; it screams through the speakers, "I've got a new gospel song to play tonight when the spirit moves on me." The electric bass player is unmoved by Matt's gymnastic display and sits quietly replacing a broken string.

At 7:10 there is still no visible sign that anyone has come to church tonight for a serpent- and fire-handling service. Sherman plays half a verse of "Amazing Grace" and, stopping abruptly, asks for the remaining changes. I reach for my note log and start counting—five men, eight women, and eleven children. Sherman walks up to the microphone, casually telling everyone that "it's time to begin—it's time to get your minds on the Lord." Without a further word, the men and women kneel

Mark Brown, Murrel "Ed" Stewart, and Gail Stewart, House of Prayer in Jesus' Name (Shields, Kentucky, August 14, 1994), praying

next to their seats. The children briefly stop their playful antics and watch the familiar scene unfold once again.

People begin praying with their faces buried in their hands, the voices resonating throughout the room. I wonder why they do this, and make a note to ask Bruce after the service.[4] It's a wonderful chorus of *sprechstimmen* that rises from the pews and fills the room with an otherworldly sound, at once melodic and staccato, and I find myself drawn to it. "Hallelujah—THANK YOU, JESUS!" comes from somewhere. Was that me or Sherman who just shouted? The service has begun, and I note the time.

Sherman slowly stands up from his kneeling position and walks again to the microphone. A six-string guitar now hangs from his shoulder as he silently watches the last of the praying. A hush falls over the meeting as all return to their seats. Sherman sings, "Amaaaaaazzzzing Gracccce, how SWEEEEEEET the SOOOOOOOOUUUUND," and the rest of the members begin to join in. His tempo is slow and self-assured, as if the gospel song were a majestic march promising to lead its followers to Heaven's gateway. Everyone's attention is drawn to the preacher, and the anticipation of something spiritual brings an almost electric feeling to the room. Without warning, the pent-up energy of the entire congregation explodes in a frenzy of dancing, rattling tambourines, and clanging cymbals as Sherman speeds through the remaining verses in double time. "Amazing Grace, how sweet the sound to save a wretch like me."

The rhythmic pulse of the overly amplified electric bass pounds my chest; the music's volume is deafening. The music is a rousing mixture of gospel, blues, country, and rock and roll. Its spell pulls me toward the light of the service. I'm clapping and singing along with the others. I stop, hurriedly grab my notepad, and scribble down some inconsequential observations in a futile effort to retain some scholarly composure. The Holy Spirit is infectious; I feel its presence throughout the room.

Sherman's son, Matt, walks up to the microphone just as his father finishes the song. He spiritedly sings, "I ain't got no time for you, Devil." My attention is immediately yanked away from the notepad as his mother shouts, "THANK YOU, JESUS—HELP HIM, LORD!" Brenda relinquishes her tambourine to Valerie and begins convulsing around the room like a rag doll puppet, wildly pulled this way and that by the Holy Spirit's strings. She suddenly stops and places her hands on Melissa's forehead, speaking in "unknown tongues." I note the time of the service's first spiritual anointing. Gary and Sherman start jumping up and down, and the room's activities are now chaotic. I can barely keep up with the frenzied activities as I take photographs. I wonder, is the music driving the service or is the Holy Spirit propelling the music?

It seems like only a second has passed since I last looked up from my notepad, and now Wayne is carrying three big black serpents, each as

Page 9: Sherman Ward, Church of the True Jesus Christ (Ross Point, Kentucky, June 13, 1993)

8

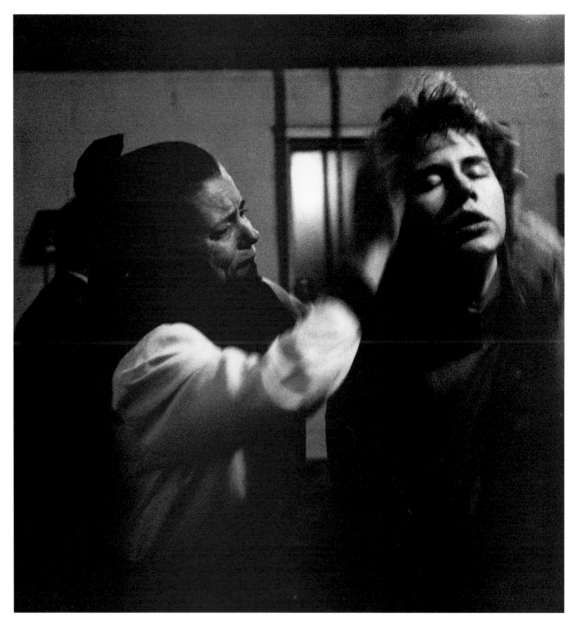

Page 10: Wayne Ray, True Tabernacle of Jesus Christ (Middlesboro, Kentucky, August 22, 1993), serpent handling

Brenda Middleton and Melissa Ward Addington, Church of the True Jesus Christ (Ross Point, Kentucky, February 14, 1993), laying on of hands

thick as a man's forearm. Sherman reaches into a box behind the pulpit and pulls out a smaller one. He raises the serpent above his head and fearlessly stares straight into its coal-black eyes. Kimberly walks to the front of the church and gently handles a big reptile with her husband, Gary. Sherman ignites a kerosene-filled Coke bottle and continues to jump up and down. The floor shakes with each bounce, and the flames from the kerosene lamp lick his perspiration-soaked chin. He passes the serpent to Wayne. From the back of the church, Wayne's two daughters strain to get a better view of their father. Their mother, Sheila, restrains them for their own protection. Note taking is futile; I just sit and watch the activities, dumbfounded.

Contemplating the night's events, I notice a blond-headed boy, Paul, standing on the pew next to me. He's mesmerized just as I am. All of a sudden two young boys climb over the row of seats in front of us and wrestle Paul to the floor. A hickory switch blurs in front of me, and I'm abruptly brought back to reality. I pick up my camera again and snap a photograph of Cody standing by himself and playing with a toy rubber snake, imitating his father's serpent handling at the front of the church. Brook is holding Sherman's hand now and vigorously rattling her tambourine. Her blond pigtails bounce in time with the music.

I suddenly realize that Bruce has taken the microphone and is propelling the gathering with another song. The different elements of the service are beginning to blur together. Now Bruce is handling serpents, and Mark is quietly sitting on the sidelines running the flame from the kerosene-filled Coke bottle under his hand. His wife and daughter sit next to him and watch. A single sixty-watt light bulb eerily illuminates the room, bathing everyone in a purifying light. Buffy, Brenda, and Valerie are now singing Dorothy Eldridge's "He Is Jehovah." Buffy's lead is natural as she reaches into the depths of her inner spirit to bring a personal message to the service. Her voice is a gutsy mixture of Joshua Redman soul and Alison Krauss country. The sound is pure platinum.

Michelle is feeding Gerber's chicken noodle dinner to her son Nathan at the back of the church, as if they were on a spring picnic. Marshall is talking intimately with Brenda's daughter, their heads gently touching. Sherman's hands are engulfed in the flames of another

Kimberly and Gary Joseph, Church of the True Jesus Christ (Ross Point, Kentucky, May 23, 1993), serpent handling

Sherman Ward, Church of the True Jesus Christ (Ross Point, Kentucky, March 28, 1993), fire handling

kerosene-filled Coke bottle that is on the pulpit. Kimberly sits in quiet reflection. Sherman's mother, Bertha, standing next to the front door, is experiencing a gentler form of the Holy Spirit. Gail's anguished expression of the spiritual experience is oddly reflected in her tears of joy. The sweat pours from Sherman's forehead and Gary's once neatly pressed shirt is now soaked and untucked. The music continues to pound my chest, and goose bumps shoot up my spine.

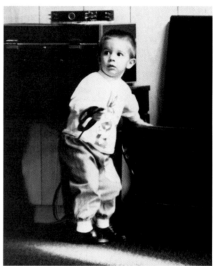

Cody Coots, True Tabernacle of Jesus Christ (Middlesboro, Kentucky, August 17, 1994), playing with a toy rubber snake

Left: Valerie Ward and Gary Joseph, Church of the True Jesus Christ (Ross Point, Kentucky, April 9, 1993), singing a gospel song

Page 15: Sherman Ward, Brook Ward, and Gary Joseph, Church of the True Jesus Christ (Ross Point, Kentucky, May 23, 1993), granddaughter singing and dancing with her grandfather

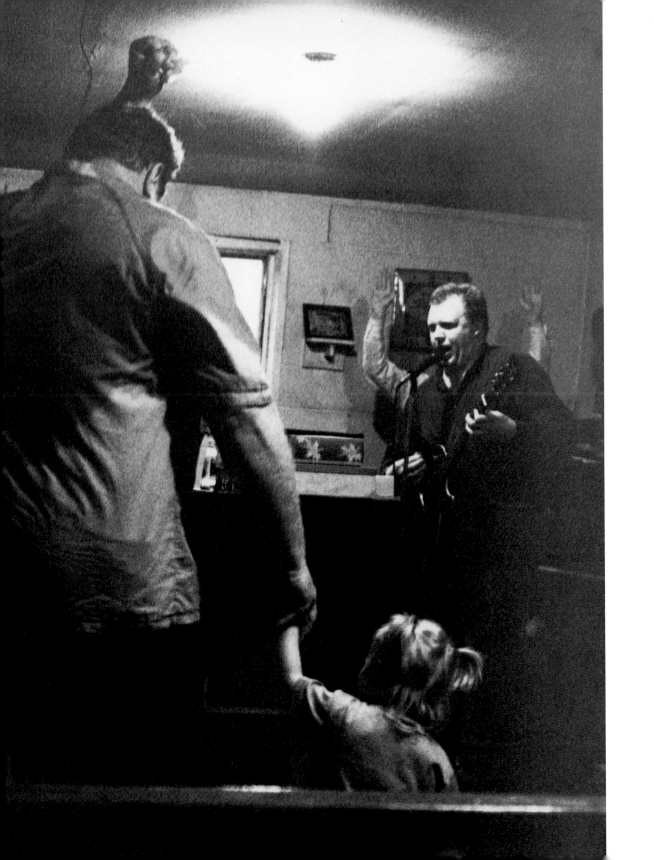

Michelle and Nathan Brown, True Tabernacle of Jesus Christ (Middlesboro, Kentucky, August 17, 1994), mother feeding her son

Mark Ward, Church of the True Jesus Christ (Ross Point, Kentucky, May 23, 1993), fire handling

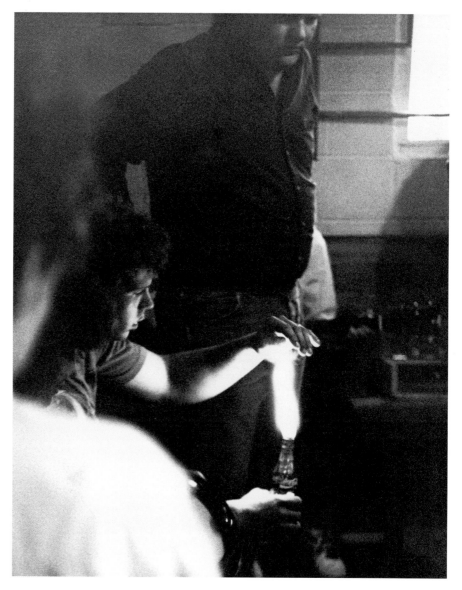

Without warning, Valerie walks to the back of the church and climbs over several individuals in an effort to reach me. She's on a quest, and there is no turning back. She places her cold hand on my forehead and begins speaking: "Sha-la-la-la-la-na-na help him, Lord, to see the way, sha-la-la-la-la-la-na-na-na." The music suddenly stops and everyone's attention goes to the back of the church. Sitting perfectly still, my ears

16

Brook Ward, Church of the True Jesus Christ (Ross Point, Kentucky, May 23, 1993), accompanying the singing of a gospel song

burning, I try to remember why I started this research, noting to myself that they hadn't mentioned anything like this to me when I was in graduate school. The room is deadly still as Valerie continues to speak in tongues. "HELP HER, SWEET JESUS" comes from the front of the church, but I don't look up, fearful of disturbing the moment. "Sha-la-la-la-la-na-na help him, Lord, to see the way, help us teach him the way of the Lord."

As suddenly as the service began, it stops. It's the halftime break of a spiritual event in which the contestants are saints and sinners, and the prize is salvation. Sherman walks to the cooler to fill up his paper cup with water. Valerie pulls some Kleenex from a box on the pulpit and wipes her forehead. Wayne takes his daughter, Samantha, to the bathroom. Oddly, my heart is still pounding, and my ears continue to burn. Several of the women are sitting on the front pew combing their hair and drying their faces with a white towel. The mood is almost jovial. Gary crosses the room and slaps Sherman on the back, proudly stating, "The Spirit is really with us tonight." "Yes, the Spirit is with us tonight, Brother Gary," says Sherman. "Why don't you do the reading for us, Brother Gary?"

Without further prompting, Gary walks to the pulpit and grabs both sides of it with his hands. He begins the sermon by reading Mark 16: 17–18: "And these signs shall follow them that believe; In my name shall they cast out devils; they shall speak with new tongues; They shall take up serpents; and if they drink any deadly thing, it shall not hurt them; they shall lay hands on the sick, and they shall recover." Gary pauses briefly, takes in a deep breath, and then, looking up from the biblical scripture, points a finger directly at me and says, "You better get right with God, because the Day of Judgment is near." As I quietly stare back at Gary, I remind myself that there's no way of avoiding the direction of tonight's sermon. I'm going to be its focus. So much for playing the role of an unobtrusive observer.

Gary's sermon consists of short extemporaneous phrases, each punctuated with a violent exhalation, the combination of which creates a perpetual asymmetrical pattern of sounds. It was the same pattern that I had heard on many past visits. "You better get right with the Lord—ha!, because the Day of Judgment is near—ha!, if you don't see the light, Brother Sherman—ha!, you're never goin' receive the keys to the Almighty Kingdom—ha!, you better get right with the Lord—ha!, because if you don't you're goin' to burn in Hell's almighty fire—ha!, you never felt a fire like this, Brother Sherman—ha!, not everyone is goin' to Heaven, Brother Sherman—ha!, but I know I'm goin' to Heaven, because I'm right with the Lord—ha!, the Lord isn't goin' to let just anyone into Heaven, Brother Sherman—ha!, and you can bet that some of us here tonight aren't goin' to be standin' at the Pearly Gates when Judgment Day comes—ha!" "HELP HIM, SWEET JESUS" comes from somewhere at the front of the church, and Gary slaps his hand down on the Bible and continues his feverish pitch. "You better get right with God—ha!, because the JUDGMENT DAY IS NEAR—YES, IT IS!"

The sermon is mind numbing, so I reach for my log and start scrib-

Page 19: Gary Joseph, Church of the True Jesus Christ (Ross Point, Kentucky, February 14, 1993), preaching the gospel

18

bling thoughts about the night's service. As I become engrossed in my note taking, Gary's sermon fades into a distant drone, and for a few minutes I find my thoughts drifting freely. As I look up from my notebook, I notice that Valerie is sitting at the front of the church fanning herself with a piece of paper. She also appears to be lost in some distant thought. Her daughter Melissa is sitting next to her, and is rocking her own daughter, Jessica, to sleep. Wayne walks back into the church with Samantha and takes a seat next to his wife, Sheila. Katrina watches her brother Cody play with the cymbals, giving him a look that any sister would give to a brother. When I turn my attention back to the pulpit, Sherman is giving the sermon, the subject of which is now serpent handling; I am no longer the focus. I whisper to myself, "Thank God for small miracles. Maybe the Spirit does work in mysterious ways."

The clock reads 8:45, and there's no sign of an end to the sermon. The communion and foot washing are going to extend the service well beyond 9:00 this evening. I hope that I can stay awake for the long drive home tonight. No sooner do I note the time in my log than the sermon is finished. Gary and Sherman are carrying a small wooden table and two chairs to the center of the room, and everything seems improvisatory. I wonder whether this is the case with every communion and foot washing. I note the time as 8:57, but I'm no longer sure what is real time and what is spiritual time. Saltine crackers have been broken up and placed on a paper plate and a glass of blood-red wine has been poured from an unlabeled gallon jug.

Sherman and Gary lift up the goblet of wine and plate of crackers and pray, "Thank you, sweet Jesus, for the food that we're about to take." The mood again is jovial, with Valerie and Brenda sitting at the table as if it were a Sunday afternoon dinner. They gently retrieve a piece of cracker from the sacramental plate, then bow their heads as Sherman and Gary recite: "Take this bread, for it is the body of Christ, and drink this wine, for it is the blood of Christ." They quickly chew their saltine wafers and take a sip from the plastic chalice. Brenda looks up and smiles. Valerie wipes away tears of joy with the palms of her hands. The scene is repeated as first the women are served and then the men.

The children are last, and Gary's eight-year-old son, Adam, sits

Page 20: Wayne Ray, Gary Joseph, and Sherman Ward, Church of the True Jesus Christ (Ross Point, Kentucky, July 11, 1993), praying over the sacrament

Adam Joseph, Church of the True Jesus Christ (Ross Point, Kentucky, June 13, 1993), foot washing

proudly in the place of honor. It's his first communion, and he clearly likes the attention. He mimics exactly what he saw his father and mother do a few minutes earlier. The cracker goes down with a smile, but the wine elicits a pained expression, and he sputters, "I thought this was going to taste like grape juice." Adam wipes his tongue with his shirt sleeve, and everyone starts laughing.

Without a further word, Wayne begins hanging a cloth from a metal clothesline that has been stretched right down the middle of the church. As Sherman and Gary move the communion table and chairs behind the pulpit, Wayne carefully attaches wooden clothespins to the handmade blanket, and I ask Sherman why this is being done. He smiles and says, "Men and women are not permitted to wash each other's feet in public. The blanket separates us during the footwashing. You'll have to remain on this side of the blanket with the men." As I give Sherman an understanding nod, I notice Gary pulling some clear plastic gallon jugs filled with water from under the front pew. Wayne hands out a plastic wash basin and a couple of towels to the women on the other side of the blan-

Page 22: Sherman Ward, Church of the True Jesus Christ (Ross Point, Kentucky, June 13, 1993), foot washing

Samantha Michelle Ray, Church of the True Jesus Christ (Ross Point, Kentucky, April 9, 1993)

ket wall. Sherman sits down on one of the pews and begins taking off his shoes and socks. He looks up at me and says, "Foot washing teaches us humility. Would you like to join us?"[5]

I politely excuse myself from the activity by suggesting that I need to stand on the back pew to get a better angle for my photographs. Everyone has bare feet, as if it were a sweltering August afternoon, even though the temperature outside is well below freezing. The heaters, however, keep us warm and comfortable.

Sherman places his feet in the basin of water. The rest of the men kneel around him and begin washing his feet. He leans his large frame back and reaches his arms skyward as if trying to touch the Holy Spirit. "THANK YOU, SWEET JESUS; ooooooh thank you, thank you, Jesus." His eyes are transfixed on something in the distance, and a tear begins a gentle descent down his fleshy cheek. Giggles come from the other side of the blanket, and suddenly someone shouts, "SHA-LA-LA-LA-NA-NA-NA," and then begins to cry. Brook peeks her head from behind the cloth wall and flashes her father a sheepish grin before disappearing behind the blanket again. I turn my attention back to Sherman, and, just as I take his photograph, I say to myself, "If I didn't know better I would think he has actually been touched by the Holy Spirit." There's a special glow surrounding his face as I snap his picture, and I turn the camera around to see if I've smudged the lens, but it's perfectly clean. I rub the exhaustion from my eyes. It's been a long night.

The foot washing ritual is repeated for each of the men, and I note that it has been nearly thirty minutes since the beginning of this final part of the service. As Gary and Sherman dry their feet, Adam runs from behind the blankets and takes a seat beside the basin. Without any coaching from his father, he places his feet into the basin and stands up. His hands are raised above his head as his father's had been a few moments before. The men kneel and start washing his feet, and a broad smile flashes across his face.

The men finish their foot washing several minutes before the women do and begin to put on their shoes. They laugh quietly in response to the women's continued wails and cries from the other side of the cloth wall. Adam is sitting proudly next to his father drying his feet. A toothy smile again beams from his devilish face, and I can't stop myself from taking another photograph. He's the center of attention and knows it. Sherman walks to the blanket and says, "Valerie, are you almost done?" In a hushed voiced she responds, "In a minute—okay?"

The service comes to a close as the blanket is taken down and everyone is refreshed. The talk is about Sunday's service at Jamie's church in Middlesboro and how well the spirit moved on the service tonight. Wayne stands next to the front door holding Jessica in his arms, and it's hard for me to recognize him as the same man who handled serpents during the service a couple of hours ago. Sherman smiles at me and says, "Yes, the Spirit really moved on us tonight—would you like to come to the house for some coffee before you head home?" Gary, who hands Wayne a box of serpents as he heads out the front door, says, "The Spirit really did move on us tonight. Satan came knocking on the church door and the Spirit just sent him packin'—won't you come on up to the house for a little while? We can talk." I am bone tired and say that I need to head home right away, since it's getting pretty late. I thank everyone for inviting me to the evening's service and tell them that I'm looking forward to returning next month. As I shake hands with Valerie, she says "You come back any time; you're just like one of the family."

Bruce Helton, House of Prayer in Jesus' Name (Shields, Kentucky, August 14, 1994), serpent handling

In the Beginning

The handling of serpents by Christians in North America is a relatively recent development, especially when compared to the serpent-handling practices that have existed for centuries among some Egyptian and Indian religious sects. Adherents of serpent handling in North America trace their beliefs to the biblical scripture found in Mark 16:17–18, which was read by Gary at the service described in the previous section. These "sign followers," as they refer to themselves, strive to be simple Christians who follow God's will as they believe it to be prescribed in the Bible.

Serpent handling has been defined by church historians as a religious practice observed by a small group within the Pentecostal movement that evolved around the turn of the twentieth century. Derived from America's Holiness movement, the essential tenets of these serpent-handling believers have been traced to the eighteenth-century Wesleyan doctrines of Christian perfection through redemption. The early serpent handlers "were members of several fundamentalist religious organizations, but later they formed independent Pentecostal holiness churches."[6]

The development of serpent handling in the South, and more specifically, in Appalachia, has been traced to the first decade of the twentieth century. Whether this religious practice began with George Went Hensley in east Tennessee remains uncertain, but it is clear that some of the important elements necessary for the perpetuation of the practice had already been firmly established throughout the South. A

Wayne Ray, True Tabernacle of Jesus Christ (Middlesboro, Kentucky, August 17, 1994), serpent handling

Gary Joseph, Valerie Ward, Brenda Middleton, Bruce Helton, and Sherman Ward, House of Prayer in Jesus' Name (Shields, Kentucky, September 23, 1995), laying on of hands

"fervent fundamentalist religious community" with its "traditional approach to biblical interpretation and traditional values" provided the essential foundation for and reinforcement of the serpent-handling practices.[7] For these "sign followers," the Bible clearly provided the direction to eternal salvation. Perhaps all that was needed was a single charismatic leader to convince them to take up serpents.

A possible explanation for the origin of serpent handling might be

Jamie Coots and Sherman Ward, True Tabernacle of Jesus Christ (Middlesboro, Kentucky, August 17, 1994), laying on of hands

found in the story of a young and deeply religious man, George Hensley, living in Appalachia. Sometime in 1908 he attended a church meeting and witnessed a man speaking a mysterious language while being baptized in the Holy Spirit.[8] Troubled by the meaning of Mark 16:17–18, the young Hensley climbed a mountain to pray. As he prayed and asked for spiritual guidance, he felt the power of God on him; then, seeing a rattlesnake, he took it up and was not bitten. He later attended a service at the Grasshopper Church of God. There he testified of his spiritual experience and held up a serpent for all to see. Some believed in this "sign" and immediately followed his example. The news of the "sign" traveled quickly, and Hensley's reputation as a serpent handler began to draw large audiences to every service he preached. Each time serpents were handled, new believers were "reborn in the name of Christ."

Carl Porter and David Kimbrough, True Tabernacle of Jesus Christ (Middlesboro, Kentucky, August 4, 1996), serpent handling

Page 30: Bruce Helton, House of Prayer in Jesus' Name (Shields, Kentucky, August 14, 1994), preaching the gospel

The validity of this story and its version of the origin of serpent handling have been disputed. However, it is clear that by the 1930s the handling of serpents during some church services had grown to such an extent that leaders in various communities began passing laws prohibiting the practice. In 1936, the city of Bartow, Florida, was the first to pass an ordinance that prevented individuals from handling poisonous reptiles.

The Florida ordinance was enacted after a man named Alfred Weaver died of a serpent bite that he received during a revival service at a Pentecostal church. In 1940, Kentucky enacted a similar law, and Georgia, Virginia, Tennessee, North Carolina, and Alabama soon followed. West Virginia was unable to pass similar legislation.[9]

Serpent handling as a religious movement relies heavily on family and community bonds for its perpetuation. The ritual is passed from one generation to another through a continuous cycle in which children watch and imitate their parents' activities during the church services, eventually participating alongside them. Some choose as adults not to follow in their parents' footsteps. Others who have grown up outside this religious community become believers as adults, and their children are then introduced to these practices.

Wayne Ray said that he began handling serpents in 1984 after attending one of Levi Thompson's church services in Baxter, Kentucky. Wayne's wife, Sheila, first encountered serpent handling in July 1991 during a homecoming service in Middlesboro, Kentucky. Bertha Ward said that she was born around 1924 and started attending Luther Joseph's serpent-handling services in Tremont, Kentucky, when she was fourteen years old, but did not begin handling serpents until 1986 while attending Bruce Helton's services. Her mother, Hannah Johnson, was born in 1893 and started attending serpent-handling services in Cawood, Kentucky, also when she was fourteen years old. Bertha Ward said that she had attended numerous serpent-handling services and revivals with her mother in both Cawood and Tremont, but had never seen her mother take up serpents.

Bruce Helton, who grew up in Kitts, Kentucky, during the 1960s, said that he often attended church services and prayer meetings where both his mother and father took up serpents. However, it was not until Bruce had forged a strong relationship with his uncle, Luther Joseph, that he took up the ministry and serpent handling. Luther Joseph's son, Gary, said that he often played guitar for his father's church services in both Tremont and Loyall, Kentucky, between 1971 and 1982, but did not take up serpents until 1989 when he was twenty-four years old.

Valerie and Sherman Ward both started handling serpents in the

Wayne and Samantha Michelle Ray, Ray family home (Baxter, Kentucky, August 17, 1994)

Left: Kimberly Joseph, Church of the True Jesus Christ (Ross Point, Kentucky, May 23, 1993), listening to the sermon

Below left: Wayne Ray and Jessica Addington, Church of the True Jesus Christ (Ross Point, Kentucky, April 9, 1993)

Below: Cody Coots sitting on the lap of his grandfather, Greg Coots, True Tabernacle of Jesus Christ (Middlesboro, Kentucky, August 17, 1994)

Sheila Ray and Jessica Addington, Church of the True Jesus Christ (Ross Point, Kentucky, February 14, 1994)

early 1980s after attending some of Luther Joseph's church services. Sherman Ward had attended many serpent-handling services with his mother and grandmother when he was a child. Valerie Ward was aware of serpent handling through her mother, Agnes Simpson. She said that her mother did not start handling serpents until she had moved to Harlan, Kentucky, in the 1930s and had attended some of Luther Joseph's tent revivals at the Leggett Ball Field. Valerie Ward said that her mother also had the gift of handling hot coals during these services, but as a child Valerie had never seen her mother do either.

Sherman and Valerie Ward's children, like the children of most serpent-handling parents, have attended numerous services and prayer meetings both as children and as adults. They have witnessed their parents' and grandparents' handling of serpents and fire on many occasions. Many of these children may as adults follow the "signs" while their own children watch them from the backs of the churches.

Kimberly Joseph grew up in a Baptist family. She said, "My mother would always say, 'We're going to church,' and she would get dressed and go. I was never satisfied when I went to a Baptist church. When I would go to church with Gary, things just felt right. I could never feel the Spirit as a Baptist. Their meetings are just boring; it was like a hole. All those years I tried to fill it, to understand, and it wasn't until I married Gary and then things just fit. I tried to work a puzzle, but I didn't have all the pieces. I had to learn the pieces of the puzzle. Is the puzzle ever complete? We're still learning."

The importance of family to the perpetuation of serpent and fire handling is obvious, if difficult to define. It is clear, however, that the perpetuation of these religious practices is decided by each new generation. Those who handle serpents and fire clearly understand the dangers of this religious practice, as do their children. Some serpent- and fire-handling believers choose their calling early in life, while others discover it much later. Some children choose to follow in their parents' footsteps; others do not.

Singin' My Tired Soul from Its Valley

usic's ability to effect specific types of physical and psychological change in its listeners has been documented by scholars for centuries. However, the documentation of music's influence on the Appalachian serpent and fire handlers has been minimal. Scholarly publications on serpent and fire handling have been devoted to insightful discussions of its historical developments,[10] sociological implications,[11] physiological manifestations,[12] and personal encounters.[13] A few of the publications irresponsibly describe the music as aural diversion and an extension of the serpent- and fire-handling activities, giving little attention to its function within the service. Dennis Covington calls the music "a cross between Salvation Army and acid rock,"[14] a description which is a grievous offense against the ones carrying out these unique performances.

I consider these views as I drive to church. A simple statement that was made to me during an interview one August afternoon in 1994 teases me: "Music helps you get your mind on the Lord so that the Lord can work through you." After years of study and thoughtful analysis, I have no better way to describe the music. I carry on a debate with myself while driving on a dark road. The music is both entertainment and inspirational prose for the Spirit. Its melodies lift you from your valley, its rhythms stir your soul, and its texts remind you of your human frailties. Yes. The music is an "umbilical cord" that nourishes the body when the body transcends its physical limits for fleeting moments of spiritual anointment. The music affects and effects certain overt physical behav-

Page 36: Mark Brown, House of Prayer in Jesus' Name (Shields, Kentucky, August 14, 1994), singing a gospel song

37

iors of the serpent handlers and does so to a significantly greater degree than the music of noncharismatic Eurocentric religious services. The serpent handlers' expectations for and physical reactions to their music and to the spiritual experience are more intuitive than analytical. Their reactions both to the music and to the spiritual experience are learned behaviors that are shared among the members of this religious community. Yes! It's the music's impact during these types of charismatic services and its "bond" with the spiritual condition that makes it unique, not its tonal and metrical structures.

The heartfelt expression of the song's spiritual verse, the serpentine rattling of the tambourines, the driving strum of the guitars, the thunderous clanging of the cymbals and the seat-vibrating thump of the electric bass join together and pound your body and soul with the very essence of the musical and spiritual experience. First it's "Amazing Grace" in D and then John Brown, Jr.'s "Jesus Turned the Water into Wine" in G. One moment it's the traditional gospel song "Jesus Tells Us of a City," and then it's Dorothy Eldridge's profoundly moving "He Is Jehovah" in D. The bass pounds, and it all becomes a blur of sound. The Holy Spirit speaks through the music, and one draws ever closer to the light. Matt's newly composed "Mansion" resonates with pyrotechnic riffs that set your soul on fire. Sherman follows with "Today I Started Loving Jesus Again" drawn from Merle Haggard's "Today I Started Loving You Again." There is no order to the songs, and you can't help sensing that some greater power is conducting the service.

Thoughts now race through my head at mind-numbing speeds as if the debate has been transformed into a mad dash toward an enlightened finish line. The gospel songs are commercial, traditional, newly composed, and hybrid mixtures of the secular and the spiritual. Tempos are elastic, and every performance is unique—the music's reflection of the church services' improvisatory nature. The keys of C, D, G, and A major are the predominant tonal centers, and the punctuating duple meters are the foundation for the music's electrifying rhythmic pulse. Minor keys and waltz tempos are rarely heard in the services. I'm perplexed. Does the Holy Spirit only move to two-four meter and melodies rooted in major keys?

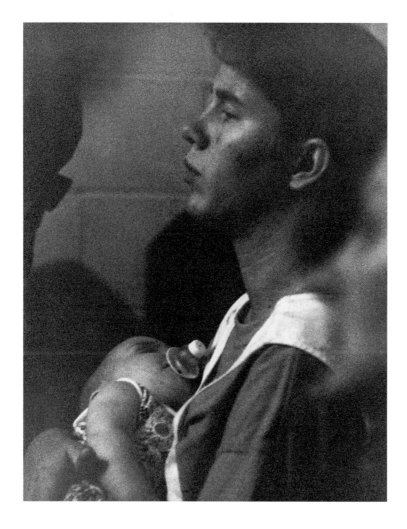

Melissa Ward Addington and Jessica
Addington, Church of the True Jesus Christ
(Ross Point, Kentucky, July 11, 1993)

I think about how pervasive the music is, about how every cell in
your body is shocked by a spiritual presence, about how the handling of
serpents and the anointing are seamless. The music and the Holy Spirit
are at one. Where does the music stop and the spiritual anointing begin?
The constant thump, thump, thumping of the electric bass continues to
push me toward a great unknown. I keep asking, "Is the music driving
the service or is the Holy Spirit guiding the music?" I still have no answer. My head pounds with these thoughts. I'm swimming in a sea of
ideas, clinging to a slippery raft that is boldly labelled empirical analysis.

When this night's service is over, I drive to a home to join some oth-

Sherman Ward, True Tabernacle of Jesus Christ (Middlesboro, Kentucky, August 22, 1993), singing a gospel song

ers. My purpose is clear. I need coffee and some answers that I cannot find on my own. My heart continues thump, thump, thumping to an electric bass that has long since been silenced by the service's conclusion. The imaginary bass resonates in my head, and I feel myself almost transported back in time to the beginning of tonight's service.

I walk up worn wooden steps. I'm greeted at the door by a man whose wife, holding a new baby, graciously invites me inside. "It's good to see you again. Thank you for coming over tonight." The living room is filled with many of my friends who attended tonight's service. Some are sitting on the couches and chairs that anchor two sides of the dimly lit living room; others are standing next to a cavernous kerosene furnace. They're talking about the new baby, the service, and a hundred other things. "The music helps you get your mind on the Lord" continues to ring in my head, and I recall other comments about the music that were made during that August interview.

"When I'm feelin' down, the music brings me up out of the valley," Wayne said to me. "The majority of the time when you're in a valley, you got to get yourself out of the valley—your mood affects how you participate in the service. When you get into the music, you get into the spirit, you get your mind on the Lord." I wonder how deep this man's valley is. Sherman had mentioned to me that Wayne hadn't been to church for a long time. "Music is where it's at!" Valerie said during another summer interview. "The music gets the people stirred up, the song gets everybody's mind on the Lord. Generally it's a fast song that works—however, a slow song can have the same effect. The Lord moves more often with fast songs than slow songs. A good example of a slow song is 'Old Zion, What's the Matter Now.' It's the text that is most important. It's the words that gets the people's mind on the Lord."

I'm perplexed by these thoughts as I sit on the couch, straining to comprehend the group's many conversations. I'm being swallowed up by the couch and by the murmur of the many disconnected voices. Something else was said to me last summer, something distinctly different. "The music doesn't pump up the spirit," said Gary. "Our music has a tradition that is passed down from one generation to another. The music fits your mood. It clears your mind and gets your mind on the Lord. Music does not pump up the Spirit, because you always feel the Spirit. Singing helps you get your mind on the Lord so the Lord can work through you. God can anoint the music, and then the music anoints the members. This only happens sometimes."

Gary's words trigger a thought about the history of music in many cultures, including its use during religious rituals. In the *Timaeus*, Plato proposed that God had created the "World-Soul dyad" and that the numeric relationships associated with the "diatonic" melodies of music (according to Pythagorus) were arithmetically comparable to the Greek model of heaven and earth. For the Greeks, the performance of music was the embodiment of this heaven-and-earth spirituality. In the late Middle Ages, the interval of the augment fourth (C–F-sharp) or diminished fifth (C–G-flat), frequently utilized in earlier chant melodies of the Catholic Church, was eventually considered to be a dangerous interval—referred to as *Diabolus in musica*—and was avoided during the early development of harmony. The music of the church was created for the glorification of the Holy Spirit, and only perfect intervals (i.e., octave, fifth, and fourth) could impart this spirituality. In the cultures of Oceania (Australia, Melanesia, Polynesia, and Micronesia), music is used to teach members of aboriginal tribes what they must know about their place in the natural and the supernatural worlds; music is considered to be of both the earthly and the spiritual worlds. The music of the Jívaro and Warao in South America and of the North American Plains Indians reflect these same types of spiritual associations.

The sound of crying comes from the dining room and a grandmother walks across the room to scoop up her grandbaby. The conversation is now on the digital recording that I made of tonight's service. I carefully explain the release forms that I've handed out to everyone. The room grows deadly quiet for what seems like an eternity. Finally, they say, "We think we can trust you to do us no harm." Everyone smiles and the living room comes back to life as the papers are signed by all.

"The music is inspirational," Valerie tells me. "It clears my mind and gets my mind on the Lord. Sometimes the words of a song fit your situation and the music lifts you up. Music is to entertain the Lord. It's spiritual entertainment." I ask if the words of the gospel songs are more important than the melody, and she says, "The song's text is the word of God." "If the words were read rather than sung during a church service, would they have the same effect?" "No! The music would not have meaning." This is confusing to me, and I find little comfort in Gary's response to the same question: "The text and meaning of the song gets your mind on the Lord, and certain expectations that you may have for a song play a role in the choice of the music that affects you."

I still have no answer to the question of whether it is the Holy Spirit guiding the music or the music driving the handling of serpents and fire during the church services. Now the matter of "expectations" has been added to the equation. Has that always been part of this question and I've not seen it until now?

During an August 1994 conversation with Sherman, Gary, and Wayne, I mentioned that Matt's style of playing is "rock and roll," and that Gary's is much more like the flat picking of country-and-western

Gary Joseph and Susie Parker, Church of the True Jesus Christ (Ross Point, Kentucky, September 27, 1992), singing a gospel song

Greg Coots, True Tabernacle of Jesus Christ
(Middlesboro, Kentucky, August 2, 1996)

musicians. I remember Gary's satisfied smile as he said, "Every musician brings his own style of performance to the church services. I prefer to listen and play gospel music in church that sounds like Bill Monroe and Ralph Stanley. This is the music that I am most familiar with." Someone else gave a similar response during an interview that evening: "I listen only to the gospel music of Walt Mills, Charles Johnson, and the Revivors. When I was living outside of the church I listened to country mu-

43

sic—Hank Williams, Jr., and George Jones. I no longer listen to country music, because it talks about things that are against the Bible."

I remember another comment made by one of the women. "Each person's favorite songs are tied to their personal experiences. The song texts remind you of your human frailties." Are these frailties the essence of the musical and spiritual experiences?

That the music can effect certain types of physical sensations and emotional behaviors is undeniable to the serpent and fire handlers. The music causes most of them to feel stirred up, full of energy. Scientific evidence has shown that music can affect heart rate, respiration[15] and muscle tension.[16] A 1977 study goes so far as to establish that the level of volume and the rhythmic patterns in music have the greatest impact on heart rate.[17] However, Douglas Ellis and Gilbert Brighouse caution that "there is no general trait of reactivity to music and thus it would be hazardous to predict an individual's reactions to different music selections . . . reactivity to music would consist of a rather narrow group of factors in the sense that a small number of closely related musical selections would have a similar effect on [physiological] behavior."[18] Joseph Scartelli states even more emphatically that "visceral reactions—palpitations, chills, and weeping—in response to music primarily occur during pieces that hold a special meaning to the listener and are generally associated with emotional arousal."[19]

Scientific evidence also documents that responses to music are the product of conditioned learning. Janet E. Landreth and Hobart F. Landreth's 1974 study of music and heart rate established that physical responses are directly linked with the "presence or absence of learning and repetitive exposure to music."[20] A 1992 report on infants and their reactions to aural stimuli demonstrates that physical responses to sound are conditioned early in life.[21]

The serpent and fire handlers say that their music helps them to sing their tired souls out from their valleys. They say that the anointing during the music portions of church services sometimes feels like a numbness that moves through their bodies. They say that the anointing feels good, that they are at peace with themselves. It protects them when they handle serpents and fire. Still—is it possible that the effects of the music

Brenda Middleton, Church of the True Jesus Christ (Ross Point, Kentucky, May 23, 1993), fire handling

Page 44: Sherman Ward, Church of the True Jesus Christ (Ross Point, Kentucky, March 28, 1993), fire handling

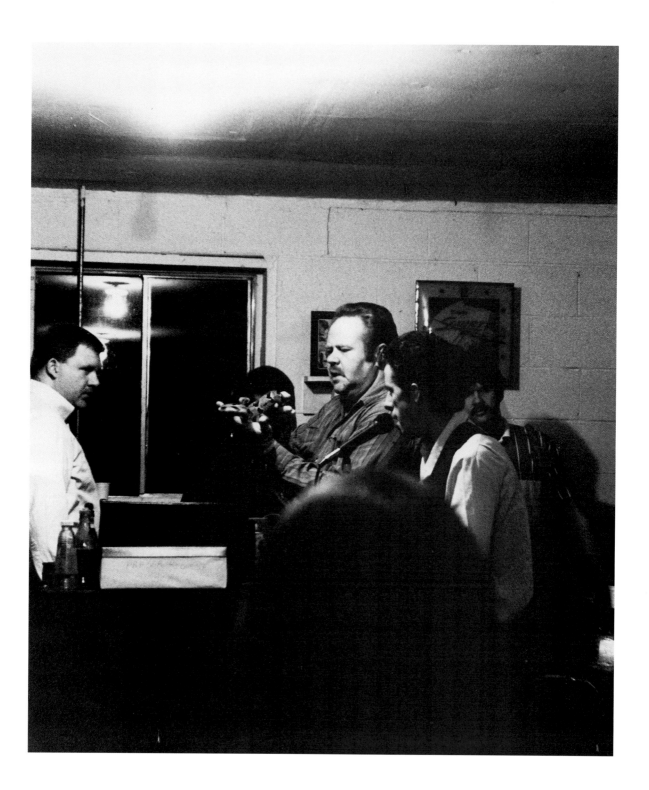

and the attendant anointing give the fire handlers their ability to handle fire without experiencing pain and physiological harm? Six years ago I recorded temperatures of fire being handled as ranging between 650 and 675 degrees Fahrenheit; clearly it should have caused severe injury. Yet no one was harmed.

The application of music as an alternative form of analgesic in some surgical procedures is based on a conditioning effect. E. B. Christen-berry's research on burn patients and pain stated that "music alleviated feelings of isolation and loneliness in burn victims and thus alleviated pain."[22] James Menegazzi's study of emergency-room patients and their perceptions of pain during laceration repair illustrates that music can significantly reduce the sensation of physical pain. However, he hedges by stating that "there was no physiological evidence to show how music had its effect."[23] Patricia Maslar suggests that "music reduces psycholog-ical stress, tension and anxiety, and as a result reduces the perception of pain."[24]

This research suggesting that music has the ability to effect certain types of physical behaviors could explain the handlers' lack of fear when they expose themselves to the flame of the kerosene lamp or the handling of deadly serpents, but it still provides no empirical evidence for their ability to handle fire without harm. Is it possible that this ability comes from the anointing, just as the serpent and fire handlers believe? I have no data to prove otherwise. I can't seem to let go of the idea that there must be more to the fire handling.

During church services the serpent and fire handlers choose to perform music that is familiar to them, and which has strong personal meaning. According to Scartelli, the impact of music on the listener is dependent on the relationship between the individual and the music.[25] An individual's familiarity, expectancy, acceptance, preference, and cultural background play a significant role in music's ability to affect psychological and physical behaviors.[26] The Landreths' study demonstrated that "physiological response to music by a listener can be affected by his/her knowledge and understanding"[27] of a particular piece of music. This supports Robert Henkin's early observations that physiological and psychological "responses are influenced by the listener's familiarity or

Bruce Helton, House of Prayer in Jesus' Name (Shields, Kentucky, August 14, 1994), serpent handling

Page 46: Gary Joseph, Sherman Ward, and Wayne Ray, Church of the True Jesus Christ (Ross Point, Kentucky, November 20, 1992), serpent handling

lack of familiarity with the musical stimuli played . . . patterns appear to be clearly dependent upon the melodic or rhythmic content and are not significantly dependent upon musical style, dynamics, orchestration, timbre, and other compositional techniques." [28]

The serpent and fire handlers say that the text and meaning of the gospel songs "get everyone's minds on the Lord." According to a 1927 study, the impact of music on the social dynamics of any group of individuals with a similar cultural background "is uniform to a striking degree."[29] Jonathan Goldman confirms this observation in his 1992 report on music and physical response by stating that "if you wanted to have an audience up and dancing, you would play a fast song and if you wanted them to dance slowly or sit down and not move, a ballad [would be] in order."[30] The serpent and fire handlers' selection of music is dependent on their expectations of its potential impact on the group during the church service. Music, serving as both a physical and psychological stimulus, has the capacity to reinforce the social behaviors of a group of individuals. H. P. Koepchen expands on Brown's observation by suggesting that music has the capacity to unify disparate physical, psychological, and social behaviors within a group of individuals. However, this is only possible when the group shares common experiences and expectations that are associated with a particular style or form of music.[31]

All of this scientific evidence still doesn't provide me with answers to my questions. I've come full circle, but now I have a clearer direction to follow in my inquiry. The continued examination of an individual's and/or group's shared expectations and experiences with a particular style of music is more important in developing an understanding of music's role during these serpent-handling services than is a study of the music's melody, harmony, instrumentation, and text. It is possible that the positive outcomes associated with serpent and fire handling, as two examples of many behaviors experienced during these services, reinforce an individual's or group's expectations and their use of particular music. In addition, the positive experiences associated with this music may also reinforce the expectation for a successful serpent- and/or fire-handling experience.

I walk with Valerie toward the dining room table, where we will go

Sherman Ward, Church of the True Jesus
Christ (Ross Point, Kentucky, June 13, 1993),
accompanying the singing of a gospel song

over the music transcriptions that I made of a recording session at Sherman's home several years ago. I feel at ease with Valerie, Sherman, and Bruce, who have shown me kindness, although their willingness to share intimate experiences with me always makes me feel like a voyeur. They sit with me as I methodically explain to them the notations I made of each song. We slowly go over the texts and melodies. They seem amused

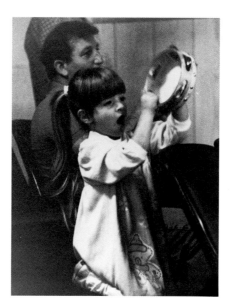

Paul and Murrell "Ed" Stewart, Church of the True Jesus Christ (Ross Point, Kentucky, June 13, 1993), accompanying the singing of a gospel song

Jimmy Turner and Katrina Coots, True Tabernacle of Jesus Christ (Middlesboro, Kentucky, September 24, 1995), accompanying the singing of a gospel song

Cody and Katrina Coots, True Tabernacle of Jesus Christ (Middlesboro, Kentucky, August 17, 1994)

Page 51: Bruce Helton, True Tabernacle of Jesus Christ (Middlesboro, Kentucky, August 17, 1994), singing a gospel song

by my attention to detail and humor me as we make corrections to the transcriptions. They must think I'm an odd duck, but they are always attentive to my quest for more knowledge.

"Amazing Grace, how sweet the sound that made a wretch like me." "No, no, no," says Valerie. "It's 'that saved a wretch like me.'" Everyone laughs, and we continue looking at each verse and melody. The fifth verse is completely wrong, and Valerie and Sherman start singing in an effort to remember the words. More laughter. "I think I've got it," says Sherman, and he sings, "Through many dangers and toils and snares, I have already come. Was grace that brought me safe thus far and grace will lead me home." "I'm not sure that's it," says Valerie. "Whenever Sherman forgets the words, he makes up his own." She smiles at Sherman as he says, "No—I really think these are the words for this verse." The loving tug-of-war persists for a couple of seconds, and then everyone laughs some more. The night is long and the Pepsi flows freely from the

Jamie and Cody Coots, True Tabernacle of Jesus Christ (Middlesboro, Kentucky, August 17, 1994), teaching Cody to play the cymbals

kitchen as we painstakenly correct each transcription. Listening to the group gathered around the table singing, I am struck again by the importance of the music to these people and to their church services.

People who handle serpents and fire use music to prepare themselves for salvation at each church service. The music is not essential to the anointing experience, though I've only seen the anointing occur when there is music. The style, dynamic level, instrumentation, and timbre of the music performance are all secondary to the melodies and texts of the gospel songs. These songs contain the "words of the Lord," and those listening are joined together in a spiritual experience; the commonalities in their lives are reinforced. The serpent handlers believe that their music lifts them from their earthly emotional valleys and allows them to experience the heavenly Spirit. The music in these services is an integral part of the community's religious experience.

A Gift of the Holy Spirit

Is it possible for someone outside the church membership to understand the physical and emotional manifestations of spiritual anointing without a common frame of reference? Scholars define anointing as the "Spirit of God descending upon, entering, possessing, filling, and baptizing an individual."[32] Believers attribute their successful handling of serpents and fire either to spiritual anointment or to an unquestioning faith in the powers of the Holy Spirit. The anointing can occur at any time during a church service and may be initiated by the Spirit in a number of ways, including through the singing of a favorite gospel song, the listening to and/or preaching of a moving sermon, the laying of hands on the sick, or the administering of a foot washing. An anointing may also be experienced by believers outside of the church service, but these occurrences are less frequent. Whatever the location and activity that precipitate the anointing, the serpent-handling believers always attribute their experiences to an unshakable faith in the Holy Spirit.

The anointing is manifested in numerous behaviors that vary among individuals and in different church services. Some receive the "blessing" to handle serpents but not fire. Others receive the anointing to handle fire or to prophesy. One believer's spiritual experience may last only a few seconds, while another's may extend over a long period of time. No two experiences are the same.

As it was explained to me during my first Middlesboro homecoming service, the anointing has both physical and spiritual aspects. As we sat that sweltering August afternoon under a canopy of maple and oak, people used the words "intoxicating," "euphoric," and "invincible" to describe this spiritual experience. The closest I have come to having these kinds of physical and emotional sensations were the times when I witnessed the births of my three children. Those occasions were spiritual for me—I was filled with a sense that I was receiving a very special blessing—but clearly were not the same sort of experience as an episode of spiritual anointing and do not provide a common point of reference.

Wayne Ray described his experiences by saying that "when I'm anointed my hair stands up; it's an electric feeling. The anointing comes out of the mouth and feels like your hands fall asleep—this feeling eventually covers the entire body." Jamie Coots spoke in similar terms during an interview at his home. "Anointed I feel like my chest is about to bust—full of energy; you feel your heart beat in your ears, you get weak, out of breath; sometimes the anointing makes [me] sick to the stomach; you feel weak after the anointing; your body is drained; it zaps everything you've got."

The anointing produces different physical sensations for others. Gary Joseph, during a 1994 interview in Baxter, Kentucky, said, "The anointment feels like you're going to bust, a burning sensation to preach, a feeling that comes from the stomach. Anointing burns you up; I feel invincible; I could run through a wall." For Valerie Ward the anointing is a "deep churning feeling in the stomach that moves to the mouth; it's a heavy numbness in the hands, a tingly sensation in the hands; sometimes it goes as far as the elbows; the numbness feels good; you're at peace; anointment feels like you're about to explode; it's a humbleness feeling, a leap of joy; it feels like electricity going through your entire body." She went on to say, "Some describe it as a gray mist or fog surrounding them with an image of Christ floating in the distance in front of them. Others say that when they experience the anointing they are bathed in a bright light that blinds them and they feel at peace with themselves."

Kimberly Joseph described her anointing experiences during an interview in 1995 by stating that it "feels like just [you are at] peace, no fears—your whole insides are crying; cleaning yourself out, cleaning out the heart." During this interview I mentioned to Alberta Short, Gary

Susie Starrett, House of Prayer in Jesus'
name (Shields, Kentucky, September 23,
1995), experiencing the anointing

Joseph's mother, that I thought men's experiences of anointing were different from those of women, with men seeming to do more dancing and shouting and women tending to be more reflective. She responded, "Everyone feels the spirit differently. For me there are no physical sensations that I associate with the anointing. I feel the Spirit of the Lord. I have no fear. I'm at peace, absolutely relaxed—not thinking of nothing else other than the Lord. This feeling has never happened [to me] outside of the church. I'm scared to death of snakes. I want a little anointing to

Bertha Ward, Church of the True Jesus Christ (Ross Point, Kentucky, May 23, 1993), experiencing the anointing

Left: Sheila Ray, Church of the True Jesus Christ (Ross Point, Kentucky, April 9, 1993), experiencing the anointing

Page 56: Jamie Coots, True Tabernacle of Jesus Christ (Middlesboro, Kentucky, August 17, 1994), anointed to preach the gospel

Bruce Helton, House of Prayer in Jesus' Name (Shields, Kentucky, August 14, 1994), anointed to preach the gospel

Brenda Middleton, Church of the True Jesus Christ (Ross Point, Kentucky, March 28, 1993), anointed to lay hands on Buffy Helton

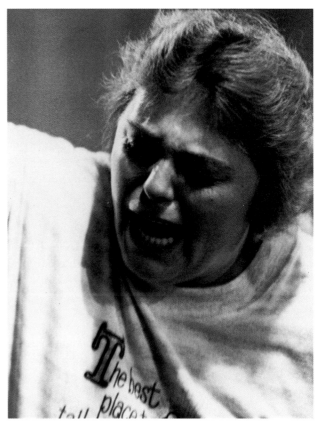

Gail Stewart, House of Prayer in Jesus' Name (Shields, Kentucky, August 14, 1994), experiencing the anointing

Top left: Carl Turner, Sherman Ward, and Jamie Coots, True Tabernacle of Jesus Christ, (Middlesboro, Kentucky, August 17, 1994), anointed to lay hands on Sherman Ward

Bottom left: Murrell "Ed" Stewart, House of Prayer in Jesus' Name (Shields, Kentucky, August 14, 1994), anointed to sing the gospel

handle snakes. I won't be hurt when I'm anointed. I don't handle serpents on faith unless it's with the anointing. I wouldn't take one out of a box unless I'm anointed. You confirm the Word by handling serpents." Gary Joseph, responding to his mother's comments during this interview, said, "Physically you know it's time to walk to the box and psychologically when you bend over the box, and you know you need to have faith to put your hand in the box even though you know you're anointed."

In an effort to understand some of the physiological effects of the anointing experience, the scholar Tom Burton and Michael Woodruff, a doctor, conducted an electroencephalographic analysis of Pastor Liston Pack, a serpent-handling believer experiencing spiritual anointment, at East Tennessee State University on November 7, 1985.[33] Having analyzed the EEG, Dr. Woodruff concluded that there were no clinical abnormalities associated with Pack's brainwave patterns during his anointment experience. A "sudden conversion from alpha to beta" patterns at the onset of the spiritual experience suggested that the condition of anointing "is a very active state from the point of view of the cerebral neocortex." The EEG patterns illustrated a "high state of arousal" that was more typical of a hypnotic than of a meditative physical condition. "A hypothesis stemming from this, therefore, would be that the keys to understanding Rev. Pack's physiological, or at least neurological, functioning during anointment are probably more likely to be found in the literature on hypnosis, than in the literature on meditation. This hypothesis is not intended to negate the experience of anointment, since the idea of self-hypnosis too easily becomes equated with self-delusion."[34]

Research that I conducted during 1992 established that the attendant physiological and psychological behaviors of those who handled fire during a church service in Baxter, Kentucky, fell outside of scientific norms. Individuals were able to expose their hands, arms, and necks to the flame of a kerosene lamp with temperatures exceeding 675 degrees Fahrenheit for periods of nearly two minutes, in no instance being harmed, because they believe in the power of the anointing. Scientists, however, do not agree and have very "god secular" explanations for the handling of fire without harm, a practice common in many traditions around the world and one which can be readily explained in scientific terms.

In the spring of 1993 I discussed my findings with a group of researchers from East Tennessee State University (viz., Dr. Kenneth Ferslew, Dr. Lee Glenn, Dr. John Hancock, and Dr. Reid Blackwelder). They suggested that the euphoria and altered perceptions of pain that the serpent and fire handlers say they experience during periods of spiritual anointment may be attributed to specific types of neurological chemicals that are produced by the pituitary and adrenal systems. For example, beta-endorphin is released in response to physical activity and/or emotional stress. Its predominant effects include supraspinal analgesia[35] (the blocking of a pain signal so that it is not interpreted by the brain) and feelings of euphoria.[36] The "intoxicating high" that the serpent and fire handlers associate with the anointment experience may be attributed to a combination of beta-endorphin[37] and adrenaline.[38]

Ferslew, Hancock, and I developed a field research strategy to test this chemical hypothesis. The object was to obtain, without disrupting the experience, a collection of blood samples from a fire handler undergoing spiritual anointment during a church service.[39] These samples would then be tested for beta-endorphin, adrenaline, and cortisol. The procedure would consist of the drawing of thirty milliliters (mls) of blood: ten mls one hour before the service, ten mls immediately after the fire-handling experience, and ten mls two hours later. The results of the first and last samples would serve as control measurements for the second.

The test was conducted on August 22, 1993, during a church service at the True Tabernacle of Jesus Christ in Middlesboro, Kentucky. The subject was Sherman Ward, a white male, forty-two years of age and weighing approximately 310 pounds. The first sample was drawn at his home at 5:50 p.m. Before the blood was taken, Sherman was asked how he felt. He said that at 4:30 p.m. he had eaten a "full meal" at Harlan's Kentucky Fried Chicken. He had not experienced any emotional stress nor been engaged in any strenuous activities that day, and he had not been bitten by a rattlesnake since May 1993. He said that he felt relaxed and looked forward to the church service.

The service began at 7:11 p.m., and at 7:54 Valerie Ward rubbed olive oil onto her hands and placed them on Sherman Ward's forehead. Almost immediately he began "speaking in tongues" and paced in front of the lectern several times. He then picked up a rattlesnake with one hand; in the other he held an alcohol-filled Coke bottle. He exposed his neck and the lower portion of his jaw to a flame for six seconds.

After returning the rattlesnake to its wooden box, Sherman walked to the back of the church where the phlebotomist waited to take the second sample. This was completed at 8:09 p.m., and, after briefly smoking a cigarette, Sherman returned to the church service. At no point during the fire-handling activities or during the second blood draw did Sherman appear to experience discomfort or anxiety. He continued "speaking in tongues" and made neither eye contact nor an attempt to talk with the phlebotomist until after the needle had been removed from his arm. The church service concluded at 9:15 p.m., and the final sample was taken 10:16 p.m. at Sherman's home.

The results of the test revealed that Sherman Ward experienced a 61 percent increase in adrenaline during the time when he was handling fire and serpents. Levels of epinephrine for the first and third samples were 79 pg/ml and 42 pg/ml. The second sample measured 220 pg/ml. Norepinephrine measured 660 pg/ml for sample one, 1905 pg/ml for sample two, and 795 pg/ml for sample three. Levels of dopamine were 1 pg/ml for the first and third samples and 38 pg/ml for the second sample. The test also revealed a 28 percent increase of beta-endorphin and a 525 percent increase of cortisol. The levels of beta-endorphin for the first and third samples were 31 pg/ml and 40 pg/ml. The second sample measured 50 pg/ml. The levels of cortisol measured 4.0 mcg/dl for the first and third samples and 21.0 mcg/dl for the second.

Sherman Ward's energetic pacing and singing, his "speaking in tongues," and his distracted appearance during the second blood draw would be consistent with an adrenaline-induced "high." Sherman's lack of anxiety as he handled serpents and fire may be attributed to the euphoric effects of beta-endorphin. The 28 percent increase in beta-endorphin may have had an effect on his perception of pain. The significant increase in cortisol supports a corollary relationship between the

Valerie and Sherman Ward, Church of the True Jesus Christ (Ross Point, Kentucky, May 23, 1993), serpent handling

Page 63: Sherman Ward, True Tabernacle of Jesus Christ (Middlesboro, Kentucky, August 22, 1993), serpent handling

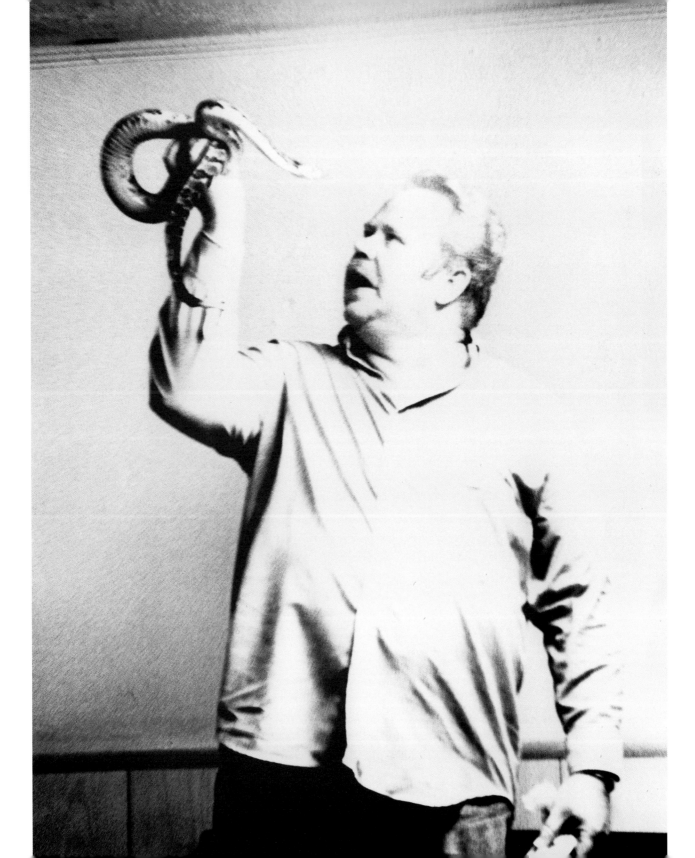

production of beta-endorphin and norepinephrine,[40] but this combined increase still does not adequately explain Sherman's tolerance for pain when he handles fire or the lack of tissue damage. It is quite likely that, given the brief duration of fire handling, Sherman might not experience any tissue damage.

An individual's perception of pain typically is linked with the degree of physical injury. Pain perception and reactions also are based on culturally conditioned expectations. Relieving anxiety associated with pain can result in marked decreases in perceived pain.[41] The feelings of euphoria attributed to beta-endorphin combined with the subject's expectations for the safe handling of fire may have decreased his level of anxiety and as a result increased his tolerance for pain during the fire-handling experience. The successful handling of fire would no doubt reinforce Sherman's expectations for similar experiences in the future.

It is equally plausible that the net effect of these neurological chemicals and other related emotional and physical stimuli could have been so strong that the message (i.e., perception of discomfort) failed to be transmitted to higher brain centers and thus failed to block "natural reflexes."[42] The perpetuation of potentially life-threatening behaviors by the members of the serpent- and fire-handling community and their sincere desire to experience spiritual anointment suggest the possiblity of a type of physical as well as psychological "addiction" to the religious experience. The serpent and fire handlers readily acknowledge the dangers of their activities but continue to pursue these behaviors. The production of endorphins may promote a type of "psychic reward system"[43] that reinforces this behavior. The combined addictive qualities associated with beta-endorphin and the physical "high" frequently caused by epinephrine and norepinephrine[44] raise the possibility that the effects of spiritual anointment, as identified by believers, are associated with identifiable chemical and physiological changes.

The results of this chemical analysis support Burton and Woodruff's earlier observations that the anointing experience is a state of high physical and psychological arousal. Sherman Ward's elevated levels of adrenaline and beta-endorphin during his anointing also corroborate the descriptions of physical sensations and of emotions given by various

Page 64: Sherman Ward, Church of the True Jesus Christ (Ross Point, Kentucky, July 11, 1993), serpent handling

Sherman Ward, Church of the True Jesus Christ (Ross Point, Kentucky, July 11, 1993), foot washing

serpent-handling believers (i.e., feelings of excitement, invincibility, numbness, physical detachment, peace).

Neither the EEG nor the chemical analyses, however, provide evidence that fully explains the physiological and psychological characteristics of spiritual anointment, and these studies do not provide adequate scientific explanation for the ability of some serpent-handling believers to handle fire without physical harm (i.e., fire has no apparent effect on the skin tissues) or for their willful perpetuation of these life-endangering behaviors. Currently there are no other studies devoted to the analysis of these individuals' physical/spiritual condition. Further scientific investigations may provide some answers. Empirical data, however, should not attempt to prove or disprove a divine cause but to provide further information regarding the chemical, neurological, and other physical effects of the anointing.

Death, Where is Thy Sting?

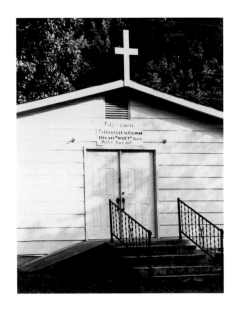

True Tabernacle of Jesus Christ
(Middlesboro, Kentucky, August 2, 1996)

Death is the ultimate parasite, stealing warmth from the body as it stills the heart and numbs the brain. Do we fear it because of its finality in the biological cycle, or because of its incalculable mystery?

As I drive back to Harlan from the August 2, 1996, Middlesboro service, my thoughts are disjointed. The words "Death, where is thy sting?" from the sermon spoken that night by John Brown, Sr., continue to reverberate in my mind. Is there life after death?

The 1995 headlines shouted, "CHURCH SERVICE RATTLER BITE KILLS WOMAN. 28-YEAR-OLD VICTIM WAS THE MOTHER OF FIVE CHILDREN."[45] "PREACHER MAY FACE CHARGES IN WOMAN'S DEATH."[46] Melinda Brown's death electrified the moral sensibilities of Middlesboro residents. My colleagues and other misinformed nonbelievers freely comment, often with thinly veiled contempt, that "anyone who handles poisonous snakes is crazy."

Death came quietly for Melinda. However, her family and friends remained behind to play out their roles in an Appalachian tragedy, their desire to retain a chosen faith going up against society's demand for justice.

Pulling into the parking lot of Jamie Coots's church for the beginning of the 1996 homecoming weekend, I'm nervous—I feel a gentle flutter that tickles more than nauseates. Sherman is working late tonight hauling for one of the coal companies, so he won't be at the service. It will be the first time that I have attended without him.

Bruce's car is parked close to the entrance of the lot, as it had been

Cody Coots sitting in the lap of his great-grandmother, Louvernia "Mamma" Coots, True Tabernacle of Jesus Christ (Middlesboro, Kentucky, September 24, 1995)

Adam Joseph, Church of the True Jesus Christ (Ross Point, Kentucky, June 13, 1993)

last September. Now, though, the trees are filled with lush green leaves, and the setting sun gives the church a radiant, inviting glow. Today is different from that gloomy Sunday morning in September when no one seemed to be able to get free of judicial entanglements and the morass of tabloid headlines. "SNAKE-HANDLING BELIEF PERSISTS DESPITE DEATHS." "REPTILES RAISED TO HEAVENS AT CHURCH SERVICE."[47] It's as if the despair from that fall service has been washed away by the heavy summer rains, leaving a delicate earth-and-flower scent lingering over the cool mountain evening.

Brother Carl Turner shakes my hand and kisses my cheek. Jamie climbs from his van, smiling, and immediately says, "Sherman mentioned that you were coming; it's good to see you again." He shakes my hand firmly, and his wife asks, "How are your children?" "They're all well, thank you. Is that Cody and Katrina—they've gotten so big! It seems like they get more beautiful each time I see them." Katrina smiles from the back seat of the van and asks, "What's your name?" I smile and think—homecoming, 1996.

No one pays attention to the cameras and bundles of cables as I unpack and set up my equipment. A young lady, saying awkwardly, "Excuse me," reaches for the two tambourines hanging on the wall just behind me. She walks back to her seat and picks up the conversation with her friends without losing a beat. The talk is casual and hushed, as if they were gossiping about boys over Cokes at the local Dairy Queen. They giggle and glance toward the open door.

I cautiously plug my extension cord into the outlet next to the wood and Plexiglas serpent boxes at the front of the church. The cord slips from its precarious perch on the church pew and slaps against one of the boxes.

During an interview last September, Gary mentioned an episode involving a snakebite that had happened when he was seven years old and attending his first serpent-handling service. "My dad was handling serpents. It was the first time I saw people anointed to handle serpents. I came into the church from the back door and saw someone get bit by a copperhead. I knew I didn't belong, [was] out of place. I had no business being up front with the serpent handlers."

The dobro-like riffs coming from Cam's guitar pull my attention back to the present; the sounds seem more appropriate for a steamy midnight dance at a local bar than for a spiritual encounter in church. Everyone is seated. I make a final check of the equipment and note in my log that there are ten men, nine women, and three children at 7:10 p.m. I wonder what impact Melinda's death will have on this weekend's homecoming. It's hard to say how things will go, but, judging by the number of serpents that are boxed up at the front of the church—ten or eleven if I counted correctly—a large turnout is expected this weekend.

Everything stops abruptly as Punkin Brown, Melinda's husband, comes through the back door. As he walks to the front of the church, he is hugged and kissed by many of the men, their strong arms embracing him and their hands slapping his back in a comforting sort of way. It's 7:15 p.m.—now the service will begin. What must he be feeling tonight?

Gary's eight-year-old son, Adam, is the only one who has ever mentioned to me that he is afraid of what his dad and mom do during the church services. He said in last September's interview, "I'm afraid that Daddy will get burned and die when he handles fire in church. When I was burned while riding a motorcycle it hurt; the pain was fast. I can't handle fire because I'm too little. Daddy can handle fire because he is older than me; Daddy is smarter than me. That's why I can't handle fire."

Looking up from my notepad, I notice the same young lady who retrieved the tambourines from the back wall sitting with her foot resting on the pew in front of her. It is an unusually casual, almost tomboyish, way for her to sit; she's wearing purple-colored toenail polish, a sort of Nehi grape shade, and her feet are moving to the beat of the tambourines and cymbals.[48] Cody plays with his matchbox cars on the pew next to her. Katrina flits from one lap to another, flirting with everyone who walks by, John Brown (Punkin's father) and Carl Porter being her latest conquests.

Gary's comments from last September's interview come to mind as I watch the children play. "The children are never in danger when they attend church with their parents; the parents make sure they are safe. The children, up to a certain age, aren't responsible for their actions—their sins. When they know right from wrong, then they are ready to participate. The child doesn't know the Holy Ghost. Until they know, they are never allowed to handle fire and serpents or lay hands on the sick. As far as the ways of the Lord, the children won't know until they're saved—truly experience salvation, born again. The Bible doesn't assign a particular age to a child; each child matures differently. They should be treated as a child until they understand right from wrong. I was twenty-one or twenty-two years old before I truly understood the experience. You are a child in the eyes of God until you are born again—it's a growing experience. The more I preach, the more I learn."

Cam's style of playing continually draws my attention back to the service's music. I'm attracted not so much by his technique as by how he fills in the spaces between the phrases of each gospel melody. He looks so out of place. People are singing, dancing, jumping, and clanging cymbals—creating a frenzy of sights and sounds—and he sits quietly, laying out one riff after another. He looks almost timid, but the sounds coming from his amplifier tell a vastly different story. Fire leaps from his strings.

A gentle waltz, sung by the same delightful gray-haired woman who greeted me in the parking lot over an hour ago, replaces Cam's burning

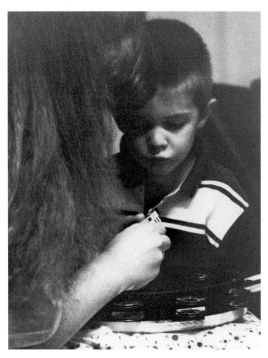

Kristy Turner, True Tabernacle of Jesus Christ (Middlesboro, Kentucky, August 2, 1996)

Cody Coots, True Tabernacle of Jesus Christ (Middlesboro, Kentucky, August 2, 1996)

sounds. Her tone is slow and assured. One, two, three serpents are pulled from the boxes. One arches itself skyward briefly before going limp, a three-foot piece of reptilian rope, as it is swung back and forth by one of the men standing behind her. The anointment is fleeting and the handling brief.

Jamie's wife comes to the microphone and sings in an energetic and heartfelt way. "Where's the tonal center?" I ask myself, and realize that Cam is valiantly searching for something that doesn't exist. All sit quietly, intently listening to her musical offering. I note in my log, "To God's ears, everyone sings beautifully."

Music and time blur together. I stop taking notes for a moment and quietly watch the children in the back, thinking to myself, "This is an unusual place for children to play, and yet it seems so natural." It is 8:10 p.m., and there is more serpent handling. Men walk to the serpent boxes, but only a few have the anointing. Several stand over the boxes as if they're about to take up a serpent but then walk away, shaking their heads. No one questions.

Katrina Coots, True Tabernacle of Jesus
Christ (Middlesboro, Kentucky, August 2,
1996)

Page 73: Billy Lemons and John Brown, Sr.,
True Tabernacle of Jesus Christ
(Middlesboro, Kentucky, August 2, 1996)

The music stops and Jamie asks, "Is there anyone else that wants to sing?" He asks several times as he sits at the front of the church thumbing through his Bible. Each time his question is met with silence. Someone suggests that he should give the sermon. It's 8:15 p.m., and John Brown, Sr., walks to the podium.

As we listen, I begin to imagine his words as the banter of an auctioneer, selling the keys of the Kingdom to those who are willing to pay the price with their faith and true belief in the Holy Scriptures. You can feel the energy vibrating in his words. The purchase is redemption.

"Salvation goes to those that believe—those that believe the most are the ones that receeeeeeeeeeeeeive the keys to the Kiiiiiiiiiingdom. DEATH, where is thy sting—where is thy stiiiiiiiiing, oh Death? Sal-VAAAATION for all those that truuuuuuuuuly BELIIIIIEEEEEVE," thunders John Brown, Sr. "The wrath of God is what you have to fear if you're not a believer." (I ask myself, "Is it death or the lack of salvation that a nonbeliever fears?") "Death, where is thy sting?" is repeated again and again and again. The words are amplified by the speakers, and all eyes are focused on the preacher. A sudden silence falls over the church like the strange hush that occurs just before a summer thunderstorm, but I can still feel the words.

Later, as I start back to Harlan, the images flicker through my mind, and it is not entirely clear where the stream of thoughts ends and the reality of the night's drive begins. A bright orange-and-white road sign, DETOUR emblazoned on its front, surprises me as I come over a small rise in the road. The word leaps from the sign's surface as the headlights strike it. I instinctively hit the brakes and maneuver the car around the construction—summer rains have washed out the road. A detour takes me to a deserted road, forgotten by the mapmakers, and, like this sudden change in direction, I am going to leap forward briefly in time to the following Sunday.

That day, August 4, Punkin Brown and I sit quietly under a green-and-white tent that was set up behind the church the morning before. It's early afternoon and the homecoming service has been over for nearly an hour. Today marks the anniversary of the day Melinda was bitten. He says to me, "I'm glad no one was hurt during today's service."

Jamie Coots's mother, Linda Coots, True Tabernacle of Jesus Christ (Middlesboro, Kentucky, August 3, 1996), playing the cymbals

Buffy Helton, True Tabernacle of Jesus Christ (Middlesboro, Kentucky, August 3, 1996), singing a gospel song

Punkin Brown, True Tabernacle of Jesus Christ (Middlesboro, Kentucky, August 2, 1996), accompanying a gospel song

Page 75: Carl Turner, John Brown, Sr., and his son, Punkin Brown, True Tabernacle of Jesus Christ (Middlesboro, Kentucky, August 2, 1996), serpent handling

Carl Porter, True Tabernacle of Jesus Christ (Middlesboro, Kentucky, August 3, 1996)

Left: Bruce Helton, True Tabernacle of Jesus Christ (Middlesboro, Kentucky, August 2, 1996), replacing a broken guitar string during the service

Page 76: John Brown, Sr., and Punkin Brown, True Tabernacle of Jesus Christ (Middlesboro, Kentucky, August 2, 1996), serpent handling

The children chase each other around the two wooden tables that an hour ago were filled with a feast of potato, macaroni, and Jell-O salads, coleslaw, spaghetti, ham, turkey, rolls of all imaginable shapes, lasagna, sheet cakes, and cho-OH-THE-CHOcolate pudding. Katrina continues to flirt, asking me, "Now, what's your name?" and wearing a sheepish smile that reminds me of the Cheshire cat. The adults sit around tables, talking and eating. Two little girls sit on the cool grass, balancing overloaded paper plates precariously on their tiny legs. All are bathed in the soft glow of the afternoon sun.

Sunday's service was unlike any that I had experienced in the past and was very different from the one on Friday evening, with its thunderous sermons and apprehensive feelings. The service began at 11:05 a.m. with a mood of palpable anticipation; seventy-nine men, women, and children were present. It ended at 2:35 p.m. with a glorious sense of resolution, a hundred and nine people filling the church's pews. This afternoon, Tom Burton, David Kimbrough, and Ralph Hood—academic friends whom I've encountered over the years—are quietly talking with the serpent handlers under the shade of the trees and tents. All are eating from paper plates and drinking soft drinks from cans. It's like a family reunion.

Punkin said to me, "I don't care what you write, just don't write about Melinda's death—don't do me wrong, like some others have done. When Melinda was bitten I thought to myself, oh God, she's going to die. This is one of the first things I said to one of the brothers. I was panicked—there were lots of things that went through my mind. The Bible won't change, it won't read no different—your faith won't change. She was my wife, and I didn't want to lose her.

"She saw me get bit many times, and she worried just about the same way. She knew not to ask me to go to the doctor when I was bit. When I asked her to go to the hospital she said, 'No.' I asked, 'What do you want to do?' She looked at me and said, 'I know what you want to do—I'm just going to trust in the Lord.' I said, 'Whatever you want to do I'm with you, whatever you want to do.' We never talked about goin' to the doctors again after that.

"I never lost my faith in God, but I felt panic because she was my

Nathan Brown, True Tabernacle of Jesus Christ (Middlesboro, Kentucky, August 4, 1996), reaching into an ice chest filled with soft drinks during picnic

Left above: Tom Burton and Punkin Brown, True Tabernacle of Jesus Christ (Middlesboro, Kentucky, August 4, 1996), talking during homecoming picnic

Paul and Murrell "Ed" Stewart, True Tabernacle of Jesus Christ (Middlesboro, Kentucky, August 4, 1996), talking during homecoming picnic

Left below: Chelsea Goff and Tesia Gregg, True Tabernacle of Jesus Christ (Middlesboro, Kentucky, August 4, 1996), homecoming picnic

Tom Burton, True Tabernacle of Jesus Christ (Middlesboro, Kentucky, August 4, 1996), watching the 1996 homecoming service

Page 81: Punkin Brown, True Tabernacle of Jesus Christ (Middlesboro, Kentucky, August 3, 1996), serpent handling

wife. I loved her. I told her I loved her when she got bit. I knew then what she felt when she saw me get bit. I really didn't know what else happened, I just kept praying.

"I really miss Melinda. When the kids would get sick, she'd take care of them during the day, and I would sit up with them at night. I miss Melinda every day—there ain't a day that I don't think about her.

"The kids knew what to expect if the Lord didn't move. Jonathan and the twins, Jacob and Jeremy, knew what to expect. Jonathan is terrified of snakes. He knows what the differences are between a copperhead and a rattlesnake. I told the kids Melinda had died, and they ain't said nothing to me that would indicate that they held me responsible for her death.

"I won't have anything on my mind, and my daughter Sarah will say something while we're going into town. She will say, 'That's where mama took me to buy a dress.' Right out of the blue.

"Melinda was a real smart girl. She was a good mother and she loved her children. The newspapers painted her like an idiot. It wasn't true, she was real smart. I wish Melinda was still here, that's what goes through my mind.

"Her dying—there's nothing I can do about that—but she did everything right up to that point. I let people talk me out of my handling of serpents, and I felt that I had let Melinda down for this. I only hope the Lord doesn't hold it against me. That's maybe why I suffered more, because I didn't listen to the Lord. I can't change that, but I hope I do better next time."

Listening to Punkin talk, I thought, "This is a man who has finally found peace with himself and his Lord after a year of turmoil and doubt." He was a very different person from the one described tearfully by Jamie during that Sunday morning service last September: "Punkin was always strong with his faith, but after Linda's death and losing custody of his children, I'm not sure Punkin is going to hold on much longer. I've never seen a man so low." Today, Punkin and I are just two people talking as the warm sun flows through the trees and the children's laughter fills the air, refreshing and candid.

The detour returns me to route 119 and the familiar yellow median. The ticktickticktick—ticktick of a stone caught in the tire's tread con-

tinues its perpetual rhythm, and the night seems less forbidding. My thoughts return to the August 2 service. John Brown's voice shouts, "Brother, read for us, First Corinthians, chapter 15, verse 55." A voice starts, "O death, where is thy sting?" "O DEATH, WHERE IS THYYYYYYYYY STIIIING," shouts John Brown. "O GRAVE, WHEEEEEEEEEERE, WHERE IS THYYYYYYY VIIIIIIICTOOOORY! Brother, read on," says John Brown. The voice hesitantly reads, "O grave, where is thy victory? The sting of death is sin; and the strength . . . " "YES!—THE STIIIING OF DEATH—IIIIIS SIIIIIIN; AND THE STRENGTH OF SIN!—IIIIIIIIS THE LAW!" "Oh, help him, Jesus!—Come on brother, tell it like it IS!" Jamie says from the front of the church.

"BUT THANKS, THANKS BE TO GOD, WHICH GIVETH US THE VICCCCCTOOORY THROUGH OUR LORD, JESUUUUUUUUUS CHRIST!"—"Thank you, Jesus!"—"Read on, brother," says John Brown. Jamie reads, "Therefore, my beloved . . . " "THEREFORE, MY BELOVED BRETHREN, BE YE STEADfast, UNmooooooooveable, always abounding in the work OF THE LORD, forasmuch as ye know that your labor is not, IS NOT in VAIN in the LORD!—THAAAAAAAANK YOU, JE-SUS!"

The room is hushed as John Brown returns to his seat. I realize that I've not taken any notes and reach for my log. The silence hangs heavy in the air. No one stirs, and I pause.

I note in my log "death, where is thy sting—new meaning." It is no longer just a series of words from Handel's Messiah that I sang years ago and never truly understood. I have only now come to comprehend the meaning of these words, not from the elaborate analyses done for the numerous music courses I've taken over the years, but rather from sitting in a small Middlesboro serpent-handling church on a summer evening. The scratching of my pen against the paper is almost deafening. Jamie then asks, "Anyone, anyone else have something to offer?"

As I listen to the silence, I think back to the time in Gary's house last September when I sat talking to Bruce and Valerie about Melinda's death. I asked Bruce how they could continue to practice their beliefs despite the tremendous turmoil in their lives and the challenges to their faith af-

Betty Helton and Valerie Ward, True
Tabernacle of Jesus Christ (Middlesboro,
Kentucky, September 24, 1995), anointing

Katrina Coots, True Tabernacle of Jesus Christ (Middlesboro, Kentucky, August 2, 1996)

Above right: Lydia Elkins Hollins and child, True Tabernacle of Jesus Christ (Middlesboro, Kentucky, August 4, 1996)

Above far right: Savannah Garrett, True Tabernacle of Jesus Christ (Middlesboro, Kentucky, August 3, 1996)

Below right: Cody Coots, True Tabernacle of Jesus Christ (Middlesboro, Kentucky, August 2, 1996)

ter Melinda's death. He said, "You believe in God so much, it's so right, that you would die for him. Your children come second to the Lord, but you still love your family—to provide for them. To have that kind of love, you've got to have the Lord. It's not that you don't love your wife and children, you just love the Lord more."

Punkin stands and thanks all present for their support during this difficult year. As he talks, you can feel the room fill with tension, a year's worth of frustrations that challenged the essence of his beliefs bursting from his heart as tears stream down his face. A voice wavering from the weight of his message signals to Jamie that it's time to move Cody and Katrina to the back of the church, in anticipation of another surge of serpent handling. The air is electric. The room feels like a dam groaning under the weight of flooding emotions. It is about to unleash a torrent. Punkin suddenly pauses, standing at the front of the church with a vacant look that's cast at no one in particular, and then he walks quietly back to his seat. Silence. I think to myself, "This man is very different from the one I witnessed last night being moved by the Holy Spirit to handle serpents fearlessly—here sits a man aged before his time, exhausted from his test of faith." The earsplitting silence lingers and then is interrupted by Jamie. "Anyone else have something to offer?" Silence again. It's 9:20 p.m., and the service ends.

Tonight's service is the affirmation of a community's unshakable faith in the Holy Spirit and the Scriptures. A triumph of good over evil, life after death—a family's and community's ability to retain its faith through its bleakest hour. Is there life after death? The answer to my question seems obvious after tonight's service. And that answer is the same as the one implied in the rhetorical "Death, where is thy sting?" There is life after death. For me it is not the heavenly sort of life in which some believe, but is represented by a community's ability to overcome seemingly insurmountable obstacles associated with death in order to live, to exist one day at a time. And that answer for these Kentucky serpent handlers comes from their faith.

The essence of these services is not embodied in a lone man standing in the protective light of the Holy Spirit as he handles a poisonous serpent. It is faith that gives him strength, and through this strength all else

Jamie Coots, True Tabernacle of Jesus Christ (Middlesboro, Kentucky, August 3, 1996), anointing

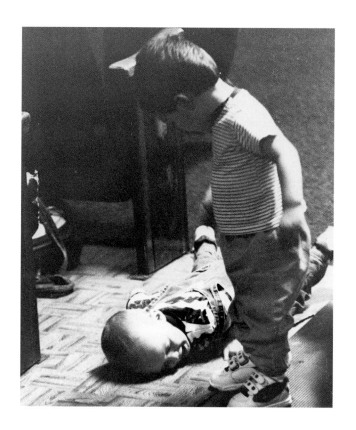

Samuel and Nathan Brown, True Tabernacle of Jesus Christ (Middlesboro, Kentucky, August 3, 1996)

is possible. The essence of these services is found in the people and their faith, in the reassuring strokes of hands laid on those in need, the cry of a new baby, boys crawling under the pews, the exquisite gospel sounds of a trio of women, the smell of kerosene in winter and flowers in spring, the blaze of guitars and thump of tambourines, the multitude of expressions during an anointing, and always—the children. A small child dressed in overalls finds security one evening on the floor at church and falls gently asleep there. The church and its services provide refuge as well to the Appalachian serpent handlers and give sustenance to their faith, which is born out of a love for their Lord.

1. The terms "Jesus Only" and "Oneness" refer to those churches in which members believe that Jesus Christ is the single embodiment of the Holy Spirit. In "Threeness," or Trinitarian, churches, members believe in three distinct spiritual embodiments. Serpent-handling churches distinguish themselves as either "Oneness" or "Threeness."

2. The book is intended as a visual supplement to several of the current scholarly and literary publications on Appalachian serpent handling. Individuals who are interested in learning more about the culture and heritage of this religious practice should read Tom Burton's insightful treatment, *Serpent-Handling Believers* (Knoxville, TN: University of Tennessee Press, 1993); Lee Smith's captivating fictional account of a child growing up in a serpent-handling family, *Saving Grace* (New York: G. P. Putnam's Sons, 1995); David Kimbrough's detailed chronology of serpent-handling fatalities and the evolution of serpent handling in eastern Kentucky, *Taking Up Serpents* (Chapel Hill, NC: University of North Carolina Press, 1995); and Steven Kane's doctoral dissertation, "Snake Handlers of Southern Appalachia" (Princeton University, 1979). In addition, an extensive and vital collection of original photographs, videotapes, film, news clippings, research articles, and ephemera on the subject of serpent handling in Appalachia is available in the East Tennessee State University Archives of Appalachia.

3. This essay attempts to capture typical activities associated with these services and present them in a way that allows the reader to experience, firsthand, the full impact of a Kentucky serpent- and fire-handling church service. The various individuals' words, as well as my own thoughts, come directly from my written notes and videotape recordings made between 1992 and 1994.

4. During an interview with Bruce Helton in October 1996, I asked him why every service begins with prayer. He said, "It helps us get our minds on the Lord."

5. Footwashing teaches humility both to those doing the washing and to the whole congregation through example. The physical act of washing is not another form of spiritual anointment; however, individuals who participate in this activity may receive spiritual anointment as an extension of either giving or receiving a footwashing. Sherman says, "Only through humility can you receive the Holy Spirit."

6. Thomas Burton, "Serpent-Handling Believers," in *Appalachia Inside Out: A*

Sequel to Voices from the Hills, vol. 2, *Culture and Custom*, ed. Robert J. Higgs, Ambrose N. Manning, and Jim Wayne Miller (Knoxville, TN: University of Tennessee Press, 1995), 417.

7. Ibid., 418.

8. Steven Kane and David Kimbrough argue against this 1908 date, tracing it to an "unreliable" statement made by Charles W. Conn in his publication *Our First 100 Years: 1886–1986* (Cleveland, TN: Church of God Publishing House, 1955).

9. Burton, "Serpent-Handling Believers," 419.

10. Troy D. Abell, "The Holiness-Pentecostal Experience in Southern Appalachia" (Ph.D. diss., Purdue University, 1974); Thomas Burton and Jack Schrader, *They Shall Take Up Serpents* (Johnson City, TN: East Tennessee State University, 1973, film); Thomas Burton and Thomas Headley, *Following the Signs: A Way of Conflict* (Johnson City, TN: Burton and Headley Productions, 1987); Burton, *Serpent-Handling Believers*; Mickey Crews, "With Signs Following," in *The Church of God: A Social History* (Knoxville, TN: University of Tennessee Press, 1990); and Weston LaBarre, *They Shall Take Up Serpents: Psychology of the Southern Snake-Handling Cult* (New York: Schocken Books, 1962).

11. Richard A. Ball, "The Southern Appalachian Folk Structure as a Tension Reducing Way of Life," in *Change in Rural Appalachia*, ed. John Photiadis and H. K. Schwarzweller (Philadelphia: University of Pennsylvania Press, 1970); Steven M. Kane, "Holiness Fire Handling in Southern Appalachia: A Psychophysiological Analysis," in *Religion in Appalachia: Theological, Social, and Psychological Dimensions and Correlates*, ed. John D. Photiadis (Morgantown, WV: West Virginia University Press, 1976) and "Snake Handlers of Southern Appalachia"; John D. Photiadis, ed., *Religion in Appalachia* (Morgantown, WV: West Virginia University Press, 1978); and Jeff T. Titon, "Some Recent Pentecostal Revivals: A Report in Words and Photographs," *Georgia Review* 32 (1978): 575–605.

12. Bertold E. Schwartz, "Ordeal by Serpents, Fire, and Strychnine: A Study of Some Provocative Psychosomatic Phenomena," *Psychiatric Quarterly* 34 (1960): 504–29.

13. Dennis Covington, "Snake Handling and Redemption," *Georgia Review* 48 (1994): 667–92.

14. Ibid., 2.

15. Douglas S. Ellis and Gilbert Brighouse, "Effects of Music on Respiration and Heart-Rate," *American Journal of Psychology* 65 (1952): 39–47.

16. H. Hunter, "Investigation of Psychological and Physiological Changes Apparently Elicited by Musical Stimuli" (M.A. thesis, University of Aston, 1970).

17. A. Harrer and L. Harrer, "Music, Emotion, and Autonomic Function," in *Music and the Brain*, ed. M. Critchley and R. Henson (London: Heinemann, 1977).

18. Ellis and Brighouse, "Effects of Music," 47.

19. Joseph Scartelli, "Music Therapy and Psychoneuroimmunology," in *Music Medicine*, ed. Ralph Spintge and Roland Droh (St. Louis: MMB Music, Inc.,1992), 140.

20. Janet E. Landreth and Hobart F. Landreth, "Effect of Music on Physiological Response," *Journal of Research in Music Education* 22 (1974): 11.

21. Lynne A. Werner and Gary R. VandenBos, "Developmental Psychoacoustics: What Infants and Children Hear," *Hospital and Community Psychiatry* 44 (1992):107.

22. E. B. Christenberry, "The Use of Music Therapy with Burn Patients," *Journal of Music Therapy* 15 (1978): 138–48.

23. James J. Menegazzi et al., "A Randomized, Controlled Trial of the Use of Music During Laceration Repair," *Annals of Emergency Medicine* 20 (1991): 350.

24. Patricia M. Maslar, "The Effect of Music on the Reduction of Pain: A Review of the Literature," *Arts in Psychotherapy* 13 (1986): 217.

25. Scartelli, "Music Therapy," 139.

26. Reinhard Steinberg, "EEG-Mapping During Music Stimulation," *Psychomusicology* 11 (1992): 168.

27. Landreth and Landreth, "Effect of Music," 12.

28. Robert Henkin, "The Prediction of Behavior Response Patterns to Music," ed. Carl Murchinson, *The Journal of Psychology* 44 (1957):125.

29. Max Schoen and Esther L. Gatewood, "Individual Differences in Listening to Music," in *Effects of Music*, ed. Max Schoen (New York: Harcourt, Brace, and Co., 1927),131.

30. Jonathan S. Goldman, "Sonic Entrainment," in *Music Medicine*, 198.

31. H. P. Koepchen et. al., "Physiological Rhythmicity and Music in Medicine," in *Music Medicine*, 42.

32. Thomas Burton, *Serpent-Handling Believers*, 139.

33. Ibid., 142–44.

34. Ibid., 144.

35. David Moffett, Stacia B. Moffett, and Charles L. Schauf, *Human Physiology: Foundations and Frontiers* (St. Louis: Mosby, 1993), 241.

36. Harold Kalant and Walter H. E. Roschlau, *Principles of Medical Pharmacology*, 5th ed. (Philadelphia: Decker, 1989), 217.

37. Stuart Ira Fox, *Human Physiology*, 4th ed. (Dubuque, IA: W. C. Brown, 1993), 156.

38. Moffett, *Human Physiology*, 214.

39. This type of test had not been done in the past because of the high cost and the complex practicalities associated with the drawing, storing, and transporting of a set of viable blood samples taken in a nonmedical setting by a trained medical specialist willing to attend a serpent-handling service. The proper handling of these samples without the introduction of new variables, as demanded by medical procedure, was crucial throughout the process because of the importance of establishing an appropriate baseline to measure accurately minute changes in some neurological chemicals of a single individual. In addition, this type of study required a participant who was willing to undergo such tests in his or her own church. Because the test was conducted as a joint project with members of the East Tennessee State University Medical School, I was required to get approval from the ETSU Medical Review Board to conduct this analysis. Approval from the board was granted in July 1993 with the stipulation that only one individual from the church could participate in the study. The board would review additional requests to conduct similar analyses in the future only if the results from this pilot project were significant and warranted further study.

40. A. J. Vander, James H. Sherman, and Dorothy S. Luciano, *Human Physiology: The Mechanism of Body Function* (New York: McGraw-Hill, 1990), 505.

41. Cedric M. Smith and Alan M. Reynard, "Opioid Analgesics—Agonists and Antagonists" in *Textbook of Pharmacology* (Philadelphia: W.B. Saunders, 1992), 227.

42. Moffett, *Human Physiology*, 214.

43. Fox, *Human Physiology*, 156.

44. Moffett, *Human Physiology*, 214.

45. Fred Brown, Knoxville *News Sentinel*, August 10, 1995.

46. *Johnson City Press*, Johnson City, Tennessee, August 11, 1995.

47. *Lexington Herald-Leader*, Lexington, Kentucky, September 17, 1995.

48. In only a few churches do women ever wear makeup or jewelry to the services. In many serpent-handling churches throughout Appalachia, a woman would be reprimanded for wearing makeup or jewelry or for flirting during a service. However, local autonomy is generally the rule for these churches, and the decision to reprimand is made by the membership.

Bibliography

Abell, Troy Dale. "The Holiness-Pentecostal Experience in Southern Appalachia." Ph.D. diss., Purdue University, 1974.

Ball, Richard A. "The Southern Appalachian Folk Structure as a Tension Reducing Way of Life." In *Change in Rural Appalachia*, edited by John Photiadis and H. K. Schwarzweller. Philadelphia: University of Pennsylvania Press, 1970.

Burton, Thomas. *Serpent-Handling Believers*. Knoxville, TN: University of Tennessee Press, 1993.

———. "Serpent-Handling Believers." In *Appalachia Inside Out*. Vol. 2, *Culture and Custom*, edited by Robert J. Higgs, Ambrose N. Manning, and Jim Wayne Miller, 416–20. Knoxville, TN: University of Tennessee Press, 1995.

Burton, Thomas, and Jack Schrader. *They Shall Take Up Serpents*. Johnson City, TN: East Tennessee State University, 1973. Film, 16mm, 19 min.

Burton, Thomas, and Thomas Headley. *Following the Signs: A Way of Conflict*. Johnson City, TN: Burton and Headley Productions, 1987.

Christenberry, E. B. "The Use of Music Therapy with Burn Patients." *Journal of Music Therapy* 15 (1978): 138–48.

Covington, Dennis. "Snake Handling and Redemption." *Georgia Review* 48 (1994): 667–92.

———. *Salvation on Sand Mountain: Snake Handling and Redemption in Southern Appalachia*. Reading, MA: Addison-Wesley Publishing Company, 1995.

Crews, Mickey. "With Signs Following." In *The Church of God: A Social History*. Knoxville, TN: University of Tennessee Press, 1990.

Ellis, Douglas S., and Gilbert Brighouse. "Effects of Music on Respiration and Heart-Rate." *American Journal of Psychology* 65 (1952): 39–47.

Fox, Stuart Ira. *Human Physiology*. 4th ed. Dubuque, IA: W. C. Brown, 1993.

Harrer, A., and L. Harrer. "Music, Emotion, and Autonomic Function." In *Music and the Brain*, edited by M. Critchley and R. Henson. London: Heinemann, 1977.

Henkin, Robert. "The Prediction of Behavior Response Patterns to Music." *The Journal of Psychology*, edited by Carl Murchinson, 44 (1957): 111–27.

Hunter, H. "Investigation of Psychological and Physiological Changes Apparently Elicited by Music Stimuli." M.A. thesis, University of Aston, 1970.

Kalant, Harold, and Walter H. E. Roschlau. *Principles of Medical Pharmacology*. 5th ed. Philadelphia: Decker, 1989.

Kane, Steven M. "Holiness Fire Handling in Southern Appalachia: A Psychophysiological Analysis." In *Religion in Appalachia: Theological, Social, and Psychological Dimensions and Correlates*, edited by John D. Photiadis. Morgantown, WV: West Virginia University Press, 1976.

———. "Snake Handlers of Southern Appalachia." Ph.D. diss., Princeton University, 1979.

Kimbrough, David. *Taking Up Serpents*. Chapel Hill, NC: University of North Carolina Press, 1995.

Koepchen, H. P., et. al. "Physiological Rhythmicity and Music in Medicine." In *Music Medicine*, edited by Ralph Spintge and Roland Droh. St. Louis: MMB Music, Inc., 1992.

La Barre, Weston. *They Shall Take Up Serpents: Psychology of the Southern Snake-Handling Cult*. New York: Schocken Books, 1962.

Landreth, Janet E., and Hobart F. Landreth. "Effect of Music on Physiological Response." *Journal of Research in Music Education* 22 (1974): 4–12.

Maslar, Patricia M. "The Effect of Music on the Reduction of Pain: A Review of the Literature." *Arts in Psychotherapy* 13 (1986): 215–19.

Menegazzi, James J., et al. "A Randomized, Controlled Trial of the Use of Music During Laceration Repair." *Annals of Emergency Medicine* 20 (April 1991): 348–50.

Moffett, David, Stacia B. Moffett, and Charles L. Schauf. *Human Physiology: Foundations and Frontiers*. St. Louis: Mosby, 1993.

Photiadis, John D., ed. *Religion in Appalachia*. Morgantown, WV: West Virginia University Press, 1978.

Scartelli, Joseph. "Music Therapy and Psychoneuroimmunology." In *Music Medicine*, edited by Ralph Spintge and Roland Droh. St. Louis: MMB Music, Inc., 1992.

Schoen, Max, and Esther L. Gatewood. "Individual Differences in Listening to Music." In *Effects of Music*, edited by Max Schoen. New York: Harcourt, Brace, and Co., 1927.

Schwartz, Bertold E. "Ordeal by Serpents, Fire, and Strychnine: A Study of Some Provocative Psychosomatic Phenomena." *Psychiatric Quarterly* 34 (July 1960): 405–29.

Smith, Cedric M., and Alan M. Reynard. "Opioid Analgesics—Agonists and Antagonists." In *Textbook of Pharmacology*. Philadelphia: W.B. Saunders, 1992.

Smith, Lee. *Saving Grace*. New York: G. P. Putnam's Sons, 1995.

Steinberg, Reinhard. "EEG-Mapping During Music Stimulation." *Psychomusicology* 11 (1992): 159–70.

Titon, Jeff Todd. "Some Recent Pentecostal Revivals: A Report in Words and Photographs." *Georgia Review* 32 (1978): 575–605.

Vander, A. J., James H. Sherman, and Dorothy S. Luciano. *Human Physiology: The Mechanism of Body Function*. New York: McGraw-Hill, 1990.

Werner, Lynne A., and Gary R. VandenBos. "Developmental Psychoacoustics: What Infants and Children Hear." *Hospital and Community Psychiatry* 44 (1992): 624–26.